CHEAP/
SMART
TRAVEL

**DEPENDABLE ALTERNATIVES
TO TRAVELING FULL FARE**

Cheap/ Smart Travel

BY THEODORE FISCHER

M. EVANS AND COMPANY, INC.   NEW YORK

Library of Congress Cataloging-in-Publication Data

Fischer, Theodore.
  Cheap/smart travel.

  Includes index.
  1. Travel. I. Title. II. Title: Dependable alternatives to traveling full fare.
G151.F48   1987   910′.2′02   86-24072

ISBN 0-87131-534-3

M. Evans and Company, Inc.
216 East 49 Street
New York, New York 10017

Design by Lauren Dong

Manufactured in the United States of America

9 8 7 6 5 4 3 2 1

For Judy,
Without whom . . .

CONTENTS

INTRODUCTION

NEW YORK–SEATTLE–SAN FRANCISCO–NEW YORK FOR $138!

In early 1986 I flew from New York to Seattle, from Seattle to San Francisco, and from San Francisco back to New York. On each leg I had a reserved seat on a scheduled U.S. airline. I had met no requirements for advance-purchase, round-trip travel, or minimum/maximum stay. And I paid the ordinary published fares available from airlines or any travel agent.

The three flights cost a total of $138.

There must be a gimmick, right? Absolutely! In fact, there are three gimmicks—one per flight.

New York (Newark) to Seattle: $89

From New York (Newark) to Seattle, I traveled on the Eastern Moonlight Special. This unique low-cost service involved an all-night flight, a plane change in Chicago, no complimentary in-flight service or baggage check, and certain other hardships. But it was the cheapest fare available on the route at that time.

Seattle to San Francisco: $49

For the Seattle–San Francisco leg, I purchased a regular un-restricted coach ticket on Pan Am. At that time the normal Seattle–San Francisco fare on most airlines was $110 one way; several carriers offered discount seats at $99; and one airline with only a few daily flights charged $79. Why did Pan Am charge a third less than its lowest competitor? Because Pan Am operated only *two flights per week* on the Seattle–San Francisco route—Wednesday and Friday 1:40 P.M. departures.

San Francisco to New York (Newark): $0

When I returned to New York (Newark) from San Francisco on the now-defunct People Express the one-way fare was $129. But instead of paying with either cash or plastic (passengers paid on-board on People Express), I brandished a *transportation voucher*. I had received it some months earlier as compensation for surrendering a $29 seat on a Saturday evening flight from Syracuse to Newark and taking another flight departing two hours later. This compensation for *denied boarding*, i.e., bumping, could be used for one round-trip flight or two one-way flights on any domestic People Express route any time within a year.

Some of these gimmicks are no longer feasible. People Express has been engulfed by Texas Air (Continental and Eastern), now the largest airline this side of the Iron Curtain. And in early 1987 Eastern discontinued the Moonlight Special. Nonetheless, air travel today remains a free-for-all of aberrations, angles, promotions, specials, glitches, and scams. And for the traveler who relishes a challenging sophisticated game, they represent opportunities to save serious money.

MY LIFE IN CHEAP TRAVEL

I became obsessed with traveling cheaply after moving to New York from Chicago in 1980. I loved New York, but we had trouble getting along. Suddenly I seemed to develop an insatiable urge to travel anywhere possible as often as possible. Unfortunately, a free-lance writer's uncertain and insubstantial earnings seldom generate the kind of funds required for travel.

But travel times they were a-changin'. Airline deregulation had kicked in, engendering a slew of new low-fare airlines and inspiring established airlines to come up with creative fare programs. New kinds of travel companies came out of the woodwork; even buses and trains were boarding the discount bandwagon.

I took advantage of these deregulated opportunities both by saving money on personal travel and by writing about how others could do the same. As my mavenhood became widely known, friends would consult me for cheap-travel advice. Here is a typical exchange:

"Are there any *really cheap fares* to Topeka?"

"Absolutely. A $75 round trip on Acme Air. You buy your ticket a week in advance, leave Newark at 1:30 in the morning, change planes in Little Rock, and you're there."

"I won't go to Jersey; flying at night makes me airsick; I hate flights that have stops; and I absolutely have to leave the day after tomorrow. Isn't there anything else?"

Patiently—at least I thought I was patient—I would explain that The Airlines weren't run by Mother Teresa and do not donate lower fares out of the kindness of their corporate hearts. If passengers want lower fares, they have to give to get. Some understood, others became angry, and many believed I was having sadistic fun at their expense.

Cheap/Smart Travel explains why airlines make us leave from Newark, fly at night, change planes at Little Rock, and buy tickets a week in advance. And it is dedicated to those of us who prefer not to do any of those things but might do them anyway—if the price is right.

SAVING MONEY ON ALL FORMS OF TRAVEL

Cheap/Smart Travel is about saving money on travel. It contains information about saving money on all forms of transportation as well as on lodging, eating, making phone calls, and using money itself.

The concepts are not limited to a particular type of travel. They will save you money on pleasure travel and business trips, on unstructured explorations and out-of-town emergencies. Neither do they focus on a special destination. Wherever you decide to go, *Cheap/Smart Travel* will help you get there and stay there for less.

Travel-Industry Developments

Three principal factors account for most of the book's cost-cutting secrets: technology, legislation, and new kinds of travel companies.

Legislation has overhauled today's travel marketing practices. The Airline Deregulation Act of 1978 incited a riot of slashed fares, shifted routes, and new airline launchings from which the dust has yet to settle. Legislation also opened up the charter-flight industry, emancipated the bus lines, and created new marketing opportunities for hotels, banks, and telephone companies.

Technology refers primarily to the computer systems with which airlines, hotels, and car-rental firms make reservations, control inventories, and track customer behavior. But toll-free phone systems, answering machines, automatic teller machines, and alternative long-distance phone companies all play featured roles in the *Cheap/Smart Travel* scenario.

Technology combined with liberating legislation has begotten *new types of travel companies*. These include last-minute tour brokers, bucket shops, fee-based travel agents, courier agents, fare-specialist travel agents, standby brokers, and charge-card referral agents. *Cheap/Smart Travel* tells you what they are, what they do, and how to find them.

Pain for Gain

As a book dealing with contemporary trends in travel, *Cheap/Smart Travel* embraces the wisdom of two contemporary clichés: "There's no such thing as a free lunch"; "No pain, no gain." There are no free lunches in travel—it costs money to go anywhere, and if you haven't any you'd better stay home. There is, however, a veritable smorgasbord of cheap lunches, and you can gain access to them by accepting trade-offs of various species of "pain."

One kind of pain involves *advance preparation* in the form of research and comparison shopping. One of the verities of deregulated travel is that *they*—airlines, hotels, rent-a-cars, restaurants, phone calls—don't cost the same or about the same anymore. To obtain the kind of deal that travelers tend to boast about long after memories of the trip itself have faded, you need to do some legwork.

Other forms of pain pertain to the *travel experience* itself. Let's face it, creature comfort-wise, cheap travel is not luxury travel. Service on charter flights is not as good as service in the first-class cabin; a quaint bed and breakfast is not the Ritz. And along with sacrificing comforts, the pursuit of travel saving may entail long queues, crowded airports, cramped aircraft, tedious layovers, rude functionaries, and uncertainty as to whether you travel at all.

Each of us responds to these indignities with varying degrees of intensity. (I abhor lines; others would rather ride on the wing than inside a crowded cabin.) *Cheap/Smart Travel* can't eliminate pain, but it can help you make the trade-off that is the least painful for you.

A Word on Advicemongering

Good advice proliferates. Each issue of every woman's magazine publishes foolproof techniques for losing weight, staying fit, looking marvelous, and sustaining relationships; men's magazines tell readers everything they need to know about dressing great and handling money.

If the information is available, why isn't everybody slim, gorgeous, happily coupled, and rich? Because this advice is not "do-able." All of those techniques work, but they involve higher commitments of time, energy, and psychic capital than most normal humans can spare.

Certified 100% "Do-Able"

Disguise it though I might, *Cheap/Smart Travel* is a how-to book: How to Save Money on Travel. It asks you to take the same jaundiced consumer's view toward travel that you have toward other major expenditures. You are asked to perform research and to comparison shop.

But you are not expected to commit prodigious amounts of time and energy to this task. You need not possess extraordinary endowments of jungle cunning or metropolitan chutzpah. You do not have to know anything about airlines or geography or maps or languages. As long as you're willing to put forth a little effort to save a lot of money, this advice is certified 100 percent do-able.

Attention Sophisticated Working Broke!

Cheap/Smart Travel is not for everyone. It does not cover entry-level forms of travel such as hitchhiking or youth hostels. Unless they are eccentrically stingy, the very rich will find little here to interest them. And while the book does include some information on tour and cruise bargains, it is not for those who prefer packaged vacations.

Rather, *Cheap/Smart Travel* is designed to serve independent travelers among the sophisticated working broke—men and women who have traveled before and now earn big-sounding numbers but never have cash. These are the great washed masses of travel consumers who fall into the yawning chasm of media neglect that lies between the *Let's Go* series and *Travel & Leisure*. Finally, *Cheap/Smart Travel* is for those with more imagination and energy than either money or time, and for whom smart ideas for traveling cheaply may spell the difference between an unforgettable trip and not going at all.

A Note on Prices

Prices in the travel industry change constantly. The prices quoted here are based on the best information available at the time of publication. They are to be regarded as approximations since by the time you read this, many will have changed (presumably for the worse). I hope such changes are quantitative rather than qualitative—that is, not substantial enough to alter the value of a travel deal in relation to other options. But this is hope, not certainty, and I apologize if time transforms a good value into a non-value.

Similarly, I have included only those travel companies and fare programs that appear to have become permanent elements of the travel industry. Optimistic prognostication accounts for some of the information that has been included, and operations judged too flagrantly ephemeral or fly-by-night have been omitted. If circumstances drive any travel companies or fare programs out of existence before you can take advantage of them, for this, too, I apologize.

ONE

FREE RESOURCES

The assertion "the best things in life are free" is particularly valid with respect to the resources needed for stalking great travel deals. It doesn't take cash to become an instant travel expert, but you do need a phone, a mailbox, and a decent public library.

TOLL-FREE NUMBERS

Remember this number: 800-555-1212. It is the nationwide number for toll-free information. To perform the comparison shopping necessary to find bargains in today's volatile travel market, you have to make a lot of long-distance phone calls. Fortunately, by shopping at Boutique 800, most of these calls are free.

Airlines

Finding the lowest airfares requires many phone calls, but nearly every airline (Southwest is the notable no-frill exception) has a toll-free number. You can save the price of a local call by calling the national toll-free number even if the airline has a local number in your town. Since most local calls link into distant central reservations offices anyway, you do not forego any local expertise. To find an airline's toll-free number, consult its schedule, call 800-555-1212, or refer to the Appendix of this book.

Hotels and Motels

It is well known that the major hotel chains, from luxury resorts to budget inns, operate toll-free reservation numbers. (Motel 6 is the paramount exception here.) These numbers access central offices that can make reservations and provide information on the location and rates of facilities, but not much more.

It is less well known that many independent hotels also have toll-free reservation numbers. Most of the independent hotels with toll-free numbers are top-of-the-line downtown hotels or resorts —the Ritz-Carlton in Boston, the Greenbrier in West Virginia, or the casino hotels of Nevada and Atlantic City.

Many moderate- to low-priced independent hotels also have 800 numbers, among them the Mark Twain in San Francisco (singles from $52; 800-227-4074), A Creole House in New Orleans (singles from $49.50; 800-535-7858), and the Western Motor Inn in Denver (singles from $35; 800-892-6767). Along with saving the price of a long-distance call, these toll-free lines connect directly to the hotel and thus access knowledgeable firsthand information about rooms, facilities, and ambience. Whenever you have to reach an out-of-town hotel, consult with toll-free information (800-555-1212) to see whether you can call for free.

Auto Rental

All major and minor car-rental firms have toll-free lines. Even the larger of the junk-car rentals—Rent-A-Wreck, Ugly Duckling—have toll-free hookups. Since all car-rental dealers offer more or less the same product, this is one area where Boutique 800 is a particularly smart tactic.

Tourism Information

Calling state and local tourist information represents a double freebie: They access a wealth of free guidebooks, brochures, lodging directories, and road maps—and you don't even pay for the call. A number of cities, regions, and foreign countries operate toll-free services. Before writing or placing a long-distance call to any tourist bureau, check the Appendix or call 800-555-1212 to find out whether you can dial for free.

YELLOW PAGES

The classified directory for your destination is a rich source of insider information. Prefatory pages of classified phone directories usually include some sort of city map. In addition, the Yellow Pages generally contains a directory to the city's public transit system, a valuable item that is often in scant supply. The Yellow Pages often includes street guides and visitor information about the city.

Local Bargains

Yellow Pages listings can help you track down cheap (but decent) downtown hotels whose principal promotional push may be a display ad in the classified directory. Look for them under "Hotels." The Yellow Pages in most cities contain a separate heading for hard-to-find tourist homes and bed and breakfast establishments: "Bed & Breakfast Accommodations."

The Yellow Pages advertises the otherwise unfindable local car rentals with bottom-of-the-market rates: "Automobile Renting & Leasing." You can also use the Yellow Pages to locate bus and limo services that provide transportation from the airport to the downtown area and to suburbs and nearby towns: "Airport Transportation," "Limousine Service," or "Bus Lines."

Useful Information

Classified directories are published by local phone companies, and you never know what helpful information they might contain. New York City directories have subway maps and scarce bus maps. Chicago directories contain yearly schedules for local sports teams. The Buffalo directory includes sports-team schedules, seating charts of local stadiums and auditoriums, and instructions for using Tele-Med, a system of tape-recorded messages on dozens of medical conditions. The Baltimore book includes an auditorium and stadium seating chart, a highway map, a guide to visitor attractions, a summary of Baltimore weather conditions, and an eight-page emergency medical guide.

The Minneapolis Yellow Pages contains a metric conversion table. The one for San Francisco includes a ten-page dissertation on public transit in the city and its environs. The Cincinnati directory contains a twenty-eight–page sectional street map of the city and the suburbs accompanied by a twenty-page street guide. The Birmingham, Alabama, directory contains a comprehensive self-contained guidebook that includes a map of downtown, a briefing on local history, a summary of city facts and statistics, area attractions, transportation into and around the city, capsule descriptions of local radio and TV stations, plus coupons good for discounts on everything from pizza to admission to a Putt-Putt course.

The Yellow Pages contains a wealth of information for travelers. If you have access to a library that has a good collection of out-of-town phone books, use the Yellow Pages to plan your trip. Otherwise track down a book when you arrive.

TIMETABLES

Beyond supplying essential information about when conveyances arrive and depart, free airline, bus, and train schedules are multifariously handy.

Airlines

Airline schedules are particularly valuable. Along with flight times, they provide information about meals service as well as the location and length of layovers. Airline schedules are necessary for implementing several *Cheap/Smart Travel* fare-saving ploys. When you are trying to get voluntarily bumped off a flight (and receive compensation in subsequent free travel), schedules help to determine the most likely and convenient situations. They are also instrumental in planning the fare-saving tactics known as "hidden cities," "Hopscotch fares," and "Limited-Service fares" (see headings in the section on "Full-Fare Airlines").

Bus

Bus timetables detail locations and the scheduled duration of rest stops, information crucial for planning meals and layovers. Schedules also help you to determine the route the bus follows, knowledge that enables you to chart a course that covers the most scenic areas during daylight hours.

Timetables are also instrumental for exploiting one of the most valuable features of bus and train travel: unlimited stopover privileges. Normal (nondiscount) point-to-point bus and train tickets allow you to stop as often as you choose for as long as you want (until the ticket expires). To plan a trip with multiple stopovers, timetables are absolutely necessary.

Getting Schedules

Schedules are free and easy to get. Pick up airline schedules at the airport or at city ticket offices. Failing that, call the airline—toll free, naturally—and they will send you a schedule or tell you where to send a self-addressed stamped envelope.

Similarly, bus schedules can be obtained at the bus terminal or through bus-company headquarters. Train schedules are available at railroad stations or through Amtrak.

TWO

COPING WITH TRAVEL AGENTS

Travel agents are indispensable elements of the *Cheap/Smart Travel* picture. Although there are practically no travel arrangements that cannot be made without using an agent, categorical avoidance of travel agents is more trouble than it's worth. What the tight-fisted traveler must know is something about what agents do and how they go about doing it. That way we can make advantageous use of the agent's expertise, reference material, and computerized data without falling victim to whatever inexperience, incompetence, laziness, and avarice may exist.

WHEN TRAVEL AGENTS ARE CONVENIENT

• For most simple travel transactions—point-to-point airline ticketing, hotel reservations, car rentals—agents are nonessential but convenient.

• The majority of discount airfares require advance purchase and ticketing. You can research and book the ticket yourself, but to pay for it you have to go to the airport, an airline ticket office located downtown in major cities, or to any accredited travel agency.

• Travelers in large cities with numerous in-town ticket offices can probably get along without a travel agent; those in smaller towns really can't.

• If you don't know exactly where you want to go, agents can occasionally provide pertinent firsthand advice.

WHEN TRAVEL AGENTS ARE NECESSARY

• Many charter flights, package tours, and cruises are distributed exclusively by travel agents.

• When it comes to booking a complicated itinerary with several destinations and multiple stopovers, travel agents (and their magic computers) are the only way to hack through the airfare maze to the best deal.

• Some agents have the volume-sales clout to wangle seats on planes, hotel rooms, or discounts that you couldn't get on your own.

THE AGENT'S AGENDA

Although agents can be helpful, you must be aware that their goals are not identical to yours. Most travel agents work for little hourly salary and make most of their earnings on commission. Like any purveyor of personal services who works on commission, a travel agent wants you to spend as much money as possible. Even though writing a $2,000 airline ticket is hardly more work than writing one for $200, an agent earns ten times as much money for doing so.

We recommend taking a strongly consumeristic stance with respect to travel agents. As with physicians, plumbers, auto mechanics, and others who perform personal services, the customer pays for the expert's incompetence, dishonesty, and greed. There is no reason to believe that travel agents are inherently less ethical, scrupulous, or competent than any other element of society. However, the turbulent conditions of the travel industry do place agents under special pressures.

TRAVEL-INDUSTRY TURBULENCE

One kind of pressure results from the *unpredictable volatility of airfares.* Prior to deregulation, all airlines charged the same fares and offered no more than two or three on any single route. With the myriad fares available today, agents have to work harder for the same money. Many, quite understandably, resent it.

In addition, the *computerized reservation system,* which is the travel agent's only weapon against airfare volatility, cannot be trusted. Most computerized reservation systems are marketed by airlines and programmed to demonstrate bias toward the marketer.

Syndicated columnist and lawyer Donald Pevsner declares that airlines and travel agents are equally to blame for customer disservice. Criticizing travel agents for failing to look beyond the first computer screen for a particular route to find lower fares, Pevsner writes, "Given such greed, sloth, and incompetence in the travel industry, it is very tempting for American and United [which market the most popular reservation systems] to play subtle 'bias games' with their captive computer reservations systems audiences."

Before closing up shop at the beginning of 1985, the Civil Aeronautics Board ended agent *exclusivity,* the right of agents alone to market travel products. While few other commercial entities have gone into the travel business so far—department stores, banks, and computerized ticket brokers are the most likely prospective distributors—the impending end of exclusivity threatens to undermine the structure of the industry.

The siege mentality that afflicts the travel-agent industry filters down to individual agents. Agents working for a commission make more when they sell more, and it is both possible and legal for them to sell the same travel product for a substantially different price. An agent could, for example, sell a client a full-fare coach ticket when a discount fare is available. If an agent doesn't know you and never expects to see you again, he or she may be tempted to sell you the higher priced ticket—or put you in a more expensive hotel or costlier rent-a-car.

AGENTS VERSUS THE CHEAP/SMART TRAVELER

Because of commission-based economics, travel agents have contracted a chronic aversion to the cost-conscious segment of the travel public, which requires as much or more labor on their part but accrues them less earnings. Agents prefer up-scale clients who put themselves in their hands. What they like much less is an informed and militantly consumerist cheapskate—you—who insists on getting maximum value for every dollar with which they grudgingly part.

When People Express started, it created bad travel agent–budget traveler relations that have carried over to the entire discount segment of the travel industry. Although People Express paid the same percentage of commission as other airlines, its lower fares produced lower earnings.

Moreover, People Express almost seemed to go out of its way to spurn agents. People Express couldn't be booked through computers. And while agents can access other airlines via special phone lines, they had to call People Express on the same impossibly congested lines used by the public. Clients were clamoring for these loudly promoted, unbelievably low fares and agents were spending half their lives on hold trying to book them. Agent-People Express relations improved slightly toward the end, but as a harbinger of the budget-travel segment of their future, the experience left a bad taste.

Still question whether travel agents are really hostile to the *Cheap/Smart Traveler*? Then peruse if you will the following review published in *Travel Weekly*, a biweekly trade paper, about three budget travel guides to Europe (*Fielding's, Fodor's*, and *Let's Go*): "Fielding's is the largest of this trio, but also has by far the largest typeface. Odd: I know the number of senior citizens on the road is increasing these days, but one would think the majority of budget travelers are still the young ones, with the good eyes.

"Perhaps the book is meant to be read in dimly-lit hostels. At any rate, this suggests a basic question: should budget travel books be reviewed for travel agents? *You can't make money off budget travel* [italics ours]. It is better the agent recommend a useful book than to dismiss the traveler with no advice at all. That way, the agent has a better chance of getting the traveler back into the office when he gets a little older and decides to go upscale." Thanks, mucho.

Commission Impossible

Agents are intermediaries. Travel agents are intermediaries between travelers and travel suppliers—airlines, railroads, bus lines, hotels, cruise lines, tour operators, car rentals—and while the agent expedites and facilitates transactions for both customer and supplier, in travel it is the supplier who pays the entire tab. At least for now. Some agencies now impose a service charge on walk-in clients and low-priced tickets, and some predict that agents will eventually charge leisure clients for all services.

Except for occasional add-ons for such incidentals as long-distance calls, cablegrams, or rewriting complex tickets, the agent's services add nothing to the cost of the trip. Put another way, you save nothing by going directly to the airline, hotel, or cruise line.

Agents' commissions are based on *standard industrywide percentages.* The commission on domestic airlines is 10 percent, on international airlines 8 percent, on hotels 8 to 10 percent, on cruises and tours 10 percent or more. These are the standard commission rates. Many travel companies try to bias agents in their favor by offering *premium commissions* several percentage points higher. Most suppliers also offer *overrides* of several percentage points when agents book a certain amount of business. Some agencies function as *favored suppliers,* in effect dealerships that receive enhanced commissions for booking clients on the sponsor airline regardless of price or schedule convenience.

Suppliers also offer a plethora of nonmonetary incentives to agents who write a lot of business for them. A single issue of *Travel Weekly* included the following specials: a tour company offering double commission on a limited-time promotion; a cruise line awarding VCRs, cultured pearls, or a Corvette to agents who booked the most seven-day cruises; another tour company offering a special 20 percent commission on a Hawaiian van excursion; a car-rental firm offering a 15 percent commission on "prepaid rentals"; a tour company paying a 15 percent commission "up front," which means the agent gets his or her cut when the passenger buys the ticket rather than whenever the supplier decides to send it.

Suffice it to say that it is neither illegal nor unethical for travel suppliers to proffer these incentives or for agents to accept them. It is a standard retailing ploy to offer "spiffs" (bonus commissions) on highly profitable or hard-to-move merchandise. Just be aware that when agents seem to be pushing a certain tour or cruise or airline or hotel or car rental, they may be doing so for motives ulterior to your complete satisfaction.

FEE-BASED TRAVEL AGENTS

To sidestep the temptations to which commission-plus agents are exposed, you may want to investigate a small but growing segment of fee-based—a.k.a. "generic," "no-frills," or "net rate" —travel agents. These agents charge customers the net rate the travel supplier charges them (list price minus agent commission), adding a flat per-transaction service fee.

For domestic air travel, McTravel, a Chicago fee-based agency, rebates the standard 10 percent agency commission and charges a $10 fee to issue a ticket for a flight which the passenger has booked, $20 for making the reservation *and* issuing the ticket. For a ticket with a published fare of $500, for example, you would pay a total of $460 ($450 + $10) if you make your own reservation; $470 ($450 + $20) if McTravel makes the reservation.

On international flights, McTravel rebates a commission of between 8–18 percent (depending on airline and class of service) and charges $20 for ticketing, $40 for booking and ticketing. McTravel rebates 10 percent and charges $25 per person for package tours and cruises that cost up to $1000; $50 per person above $1000. In the event of cancellations, the service charge is non-refundable.

McTravel charges the full price of the ticket to any major charge card and sends a check for the rebate along with the ticket. McTravel operates nationwide, taking orders by phone and delivering tickets by regular mail. For an additional charge they can arrange overnight delivery; they also accept payment by cashier's check and money order. Call McTravel at 800-331-2941 (in IL, 312-876-1116) from 9:00 A.M. to 5:00 P.M. Central time.

Other fee-based agencies and rebaters operate in various ways. Cashback Travel (800-458-CASH) offers rebates of from 2–7 percent on airline tickets and a 50/50 split on hotel and car-rental commissions. The Take Off Card (800-222-8285; in MD, 800-222-7271) has a membership arrangement for rebates on airfares and other travel discounts. Memberships range from $30 a year for individuals to $145 for three years for families.

Operating from the bargain-conscious climes of the legendary Filene's Basement department stores, the Vacation Outlet (617-267-2411) sells package tours and cruises for at least $20–$100 off list price. The Smart Traveller Group of independent agencies offers discounts of around 7 percent—an average of $150 or more—on trips, package tours, and cruises that clients plan themselves. Contact Pennsylvania Travel in Philadelphia (215-251-9944; in Northeast states from Connecticut to Virginia, 800-331-0947) or The Smart Traveller in Miami (305-662-6677).

Some bankcards have new programs that offer participants benefits that sound suspiciously like rebates. For $39 a year, Citibank Visa and MasterCard holders can join CitiTravel (800-526-4848) to receive, among other goodies, 5–10 percent "cash awards" on any travel purchased through the program.

Keep an eye on the travel section of your daily paper or other local publications for fee-based agencies in your area. Spot them through ads that offer savings to all destinations, on any airline, anytime, etc.

If you have any qualms about the legitimacy of a dealer, inquire whether they or the travel agent that tickets for them is registered with the Airline Reporting Corporation: ARC registration is a requirement for selling domestic airline tickets. Then call ARC headquarters in Washington, D.C. (202-626-4067) to confirm their registration.

Fee-based travel agents dovetail perfectly with the techniques of *Cheap/Smart Travel*. We provide the information that lets you track and book the *lowest available fare*. Then the no-frills agent writes the ticket for *even less*.

WHO ARE THESE GUYS?

Apart from the commission system, another obstacle in getting good service is *agent inexperience and ignorance*. Despite the pretensions of professionalism, the agent you encounter may well be an ill-trained part-timer who works in the agency more for the fringe benefits (notably discount, subsidized, or free travel) than to make a living. Such agents can probably book a package tour or a point-to-point flight, but they are unlikely to have the expertise to use a complex and biased computer to construct low-fare itineraries.

Membership in either of the two principal *travel agency professional associations*, the American Society of Travel Agents (ASTA) and the Association of Retail Travel Agents (ARTA) is a plus in establishing the solvency and integrity of the agency. But an ASTA or ARTA affiliation does not ensure the competence of every agent in the office. One indication of an individual agent's ability is his or her qualification as a "certified travel counselor" (CTC). To become a CTC, an agent with at least five years' experience must complete a two-year graduate-level program offered by the Institute of Certified Travel Agents.

"FAM" TRIPS

Even if agents are competent and ethical, they are still unlikely to know much about low-priced travel. Aside from whatever personal travel they have done, agents acquire most firsthand knowledge of destinations and carriers from "fam" (short for familiarization) trips sponsored by travel suppliers. Fam trips give suppliers the opportunity to show off their wares; they offer agents an opportunity to travel for free or for a fraction of the normal price.

The worst thing about fam trips is that only the upper echelons of travel-industry suppliers run them. Agents fly free on major airlines and, whenever possible, get upgraded to business- or first-class sections. Consequently, they are unlikely to know much about cut-rate carriers, charters, or even the major airlines' economy cabins.

Since agents usually stay in the best hotels and dine in brand-name restaurants, they are unlikely to know much about the charming inns or hidden dining treasures of the destinations they have personally visited. And since they have received accommodations and transportation for free or close to it, an understandably human sense of gratitude inclines them to subsequently give their hosts the benefit of every doubt. (Fam trips, incidentally, are not necessarily a day at the beach. Since the trips are sponsored by a number of hotels, restaurants, and attractions—all of which exact their pound of flesh from the agents—fam trips are often one part recreation to three parts exhaustion.)

Whether an individual who has received the VIP treatment and accommodations or food for free can provide appraisal dispassionate enough to suit those who must pay for same is a thorny philosophical and professional problem. (It is equally thorny for travel writers, who freeload even more opulently than agents.) Suffice it to say that even the information an agent supplies based on personal experience may be neither impartial nor pertinent.

FINDING *YOUR* KIND OF TRAVEL AGENT

Even if you need an agent only to write a ticket you've booked yourself, it helps to have one with whom you can communicate. *The only absolutely fabulous way to find a good travel agent is by word of mouth recommendation.* Obtaining such recommendations is not easy. In an informal survey in which I asked people to recommend a good travel agent, about half said they had no regular agent; most of the others said they couldn't recommend their agents because they didn't completely trust them. (Most, however, freely volunteered the name of their accountants.)

In the absence of a wholehearted personal recommendation of a knowledgeable and experienced traveler, try the travel agent used by your employer. This may be an in-house agency—a branch of a travel agency located on your premises. Some in-houses consider it part of their job to book personal travel; others either won't or aren't permitted to. Or consult the outside travel agency used by your firm. In either case, the agency has your company's continued patronage and good will as an incentive to bend over backward for you.

Be aware that *travel agents specialize* and that specialties focus on either a type of customer or a type of travel. The major areas of specialization are business and leisure travel. While every accredited agency has the authority to book any kind of travel, leisure agencies specialize in cruises, charters, low airfares, or up-scale resorts. The advertising in local media reveals much about an agency's area of expertise.

BE PREPARED!

The *Cheap/Smart Travel* motto is the same as the Boy Scouts': Be prepared. If you know where you want to go, price a few fares before you contact an agent. When you go to the agent, show him or her what you have and challenge the office computer to top it.

Ask friends or consult guidebooks for the names of a few hotels in the area. The agent may accept or refute them with better suggestions, but at least you will have a basis for comparison. True, your knowledge will be superficial, and everyone agrees that "a little learning is a dangerous thing." (Pope) "No learning whatsoever, however, can be an invitation to a rip-off." (Fischer)

Before approaching a travel agent, you should at least *decide on the kind of trip you want.* A week in the sun? Heavy-duty culture and sightseeing? A food and drink binge? Something else wondrous strange. Although agents today tend to up-scale themselves to "travel planners," "travel counselors," "travel advisers," and, most pretentiously, "travel consultants," they are actually "travel salespersons." As such, they don't get paid to plan, counsel, advise, or consult—they get paid when they sell. Don't waste their time. Your part of the bargain is to be a serious and informed customer who at least intends to make a travel purchase when you walk through the door or pick up the phone.

There are many excellent reasons for cultivating amicable relations with a capable travel agent. Good agents can, at best, save you both money and time. They also have a wealth of knowledge—in reference books and periodicals, on computers, and in their heads—to place at your disposal. A satisfactory relationship with a travel agent can be as fruitful as a good relationship with your doctor, lawyer, or accountant.

The problem is that all travel agents are not capable. Unlike doctors, lawyers, and accountants, they are not professionally certified. They are not licensed (not yet anyway, although movements to do so are now under way in several states), and they are responsible to no authority higher than the guy who gave them their job. Given this lack of accreditation *plus* the vast amount of territory covered by the travel industry *plus* the turbulent conditions of that industry, it is hardly surprising that agents need to be closely "Naderized" and that the unwritten law of traveler-agent interaction must remain *caveat emptor.*

THREE

SHOPPING AT THE AIR TRANS-
PORTATION FLEA MARKET

THE ROOTS OF DISCOUNT AIR TRAVEL

No-frills airlines, Super-Saver fares, Ultra-Saver fares, frequent flyer bonus programs, and the like have become so entrenched as features of air travel today that it's hard to believe that ten years ago none of them existed.

Prior to the Deregulation Act of 1978, all airlines flying a particular route charged the same fares. Fares closely reflected the number of air miles on that route and passengers could choose only among coach, first class, and, on a few routes, night coach. Back in the regulated old days airlines couldn't compete on the basis of price, so they competed on the elements of the flying experience that really mattered: schedule convenience, punctuality, size of steak, and stewardess pulchritude.

Internationally, the situation was no less rigid. On major airlines the only way to beat the economy fares was to buy Apex fares with strict advance booking and length of stay requirements. The only alternatives were charter flights, then limited to the membership of "affinity groups," and good old Icelandair.

Skytrain

The Victorian era began to fade in 1977 with the advent of the Laker Skytrain. Laker charged $135 for a one-way ticket between New York (JFK) and London (Gatwick), less than half the economy fare on major carriers.

At first Skytrain maintained the puritanical pretense that airfare savings had to be bought with excruciating inconvenience. On flight day passengers had to go to a Laker ticket office in Rego Park, Queens, some ten miles from JFK airport. First-come, first-served only tickets that went on sale at 4:00 A.M. on the morning before each 11:00 P.M. flight and all-night queues were considered attributes of the low-fare experience, as were crowded DC-10s and the extra-charge food and beverages that inspired the first airborne brownbagging.

The Great Coupon Giveaway

Although the Civil Aeronautics Board deregulated U.S. airfares in 1978, the standard mileage-based fare system didn't begin to erode until the Great Coupon Giveaway in the spring of 1979.

Then, in order to get quickly back on its feet after a two-month mechanics strike, United gave passengers on every flight segment a coupon permitting them to purchase a round-trip ticket to any destination in the contiguous forty-eight states for half of the normal fare. American simultaneously matched the offer, and between May 28 and June 17, the two airlines distributed an estimated six million half-fare coupons.

Overnight a new American industry was born. Suddenly the airports' Hare Krishnas and nuclear-power advocates were joined by shifty characters brandishing hastily scribbled signs offering "cash for coupons." The cash changed hands openly—from $5 to $20 a coupon depending on how well passengers bargained—as sellers flitted from buyer to buyer in search of a better price. Classified ads offering to buy and/or sell coupons began to appear in daily papers.

American and United enjoyed a windfall of business, particularly on short flights. I was lucky to get one of the last seats on a 6:45 A.M. Sunday United night coach flight from Chicago to South Bend (United's cheapest Chicago flight) near the end of the coupon promotion. All this for a ticket good for only half off normal coach, hardly a grandiose discount in terms of what was to ensue.

A New Airline Industry

Although it lasted less than a month and the coupons had to be used by December 15 of the same year, the coupon giveaway permanently changed the complexion of the U.S. airline industry. First, it made the public aware that deregulation existed and that airlines now had more discretion in setting fares than they had in the past.

It also made the flying public realize that airfares were neither rational nor set in stone. A seat on an airplane was a commodity that could be bought, sold, traded, or given away. If anything, it was perhaps more market-sensitive than other commodities because once the plane took off it wasn't worth anything to anybody.

The Discount Generation

Today discount airfares go both wider and deeper than they did in those early years. In 1987, more than 90 percent of U.S. air travel took place on some sort of discount ticket. The size of the average discount is now a record-high 63 percent off full-fare coach.

The APEX fares that had existed only on overseas flights have, after many modifications and permutations, become institutionalized as Ultra-Saver and MaxSaver fares. Laker's no-frills international example has been adapted with more lasting success domestically by Southwest.

Air transportation has become a flea market where shoppers can find everything from sensational bargains on quality merchandise to outright junk. As in any flea market, sellers take advantage of the impatient and the ill informed. And as in any flea market, wonderful bargains go to those who recognize them and know their value.

DISCOUNTS ON FULL-FARE AIRLINES
The Deregulation Revolution

Since passage of the Airline Deregulation Act of 1978, the airline industry has been in a prolonged state of controlled chaos. Deregulation permitted airlines to act like any other business of a free society. They no longer needed government approval of routing systems and scheduling and could charge any fare, impose any conditions for purchasing those fares, and provide or withhold in-flight services. Although the government still regulated the treatment of passengers, scheduling and pricing were now principally subject to the forces of competitive capitalism.

Deregulation has revolutionized the U.S. air-travel industry. Because competition mandates fewer flights with higher load ratios, the "hub-and-spoke" system, in which airlines cluster flights to and from centrally located hubs, has become the industry standard. Numerous new airlines—America West, Virgin Atlantic, Midway Airlines, to name a few—have taken to the skies, while established airlines like Altair and Frontier have disappeared and others—notably Continental and Braniff—have filed for bankruptcy and become reborn discounters.

Airfare Anarchy

The most perplexing outgrowth of airline deregulation has to be the profusion of new fares and the seemingly perverse and capricious restrictions involved in purchasing them. A passenger's options used to be limited to coach, first-class, and occasionally night-coach fares that were identical on all carriers flying a particular route. Now passengers must assess excursion fares, Max-Savers, Super-Savers, Ultra-Savers, Freedom fares, Hopscotch fares, and a potpourri of others.

These fares drive passengers and travel agents up the wall, and their only true fans are travel-skills journalists and stand-up comics who have replaced material about plastic food and lascivious "stewardi" with wisecracks about fares that require you to pay with silver dollars, fly on Arbor Day, and change planes in beautiful downtown Burbank.

The Hidden Logic of Airfares

Actually, the U.S. airfare structure is extremely logical—not simple but logical. The restrictions and stipulations conspire to accomplish two somewhat contradictory goals: (1) make business travelers who must travel regardless of price pay the highest possible fare; and (2) create low-fare programs that entice pleasure travelers who don't have to fly and will do so only if the price is right. The restrictions and conditions are the airline's attempts to fill every plane with the most profitable combination of business and pleasure travelers.

Thwarting Business Travelers

Tracking the behavior of business passengers (and thus thwarting their quest for discounts) has been facilitated by the creation of frequent-flyer clubs. The airlines not only know the names and addresses of their best customers but exactly when, where, what time of day, and how frequently they travel. By analyzing these travel patterns, airlines have determined precisely which restrictions business passengers can least easily accommodate and have structured discount programs accordingly:

● Business travelers must often travel at the last minute and do not always know how long they will be gone. Consequently, discount fares carry advance-purchase and booking requirements ranging from three to thirty days prior to departure. As a rule, the farther ahead you pay, the cheaper the ticket will be.
● Because business travelers fly during the week and return home for weekends, discount fares usually require round-trip travel and a weekend stay.
● Since Monday, Friday, and Sunday are the heaviest days for both business and pleasure passengers, discretionary travelers can get lower fares by flying on Tuesday, Wednesday, Thursday, or Saturday.

Airfares may seem arbitrary, but their logic is based on hard computer-generated data. Moreover, competitive pressures and changing economic conditions further confound the situation and force airlines to alter fares at the pace of an estimated *76,000 changes every day*. And although airlines constantly strive to stabilize fares according to an intelligible mileage-based formula, this stabilization has yet to materialize. What *Cheap/Smart Travel* can do is outline the shape of the principal discount programs and detail the techniques for ferreting out low fares from wherever they may be hiding.

The Full-Fare Airlines

The fares programs and procedures apply to the full-fare, full-service U.S. airlines that serve most major U.S. markets. These carriers gear discounts to a standard coach (Y) fare, provide first-class and coach service, serve free meals and beverages, and maintain interlining agreements that permit baggage transfer between connecting flights and common ticketing.

Under these criteria, the major airlines include American, Eastern, Delta (incorporating Western), Northwest Orient (incorporating Republic), Pan Am, TWA (incorporating Ozark), and United. Other airlines that have similar ticketing and service policies but operate on a regional basis include Piedmont and US Air, which are in the process of merging.

Full-fare airlines structure their fares according to a mileage-based standard coach Y fare, the airline equivalent of the automobile sticker price. On less-traveled routes, passengers may have no unrestricted alternatives to standard coach. On heavily traveled routes between major cities—New York–Chicago, Los Angeles–San Francisco, New York–Los Angeles—competition from cut-rate carriers has virtually discounted the Y fare out of existence.

But coach fares are alive and well, and if you don't watch out, some airline or travel agent will sell it to you. If you ask United for the "coach" fare between New York and Chicago, they will quote a fare of $310; ask for the "lowest fare" and you pay $99 or even less each way based on a round-trip ticket with certain restrictions.

And some airlines program their computers with a "walk-up pricing policy" under which an hour or two before flight time all fares except full-fare coach automatically vanish. Under some circumstances, the walk-up policy is extended to twenty-four hours.

MaxSavers

Texas Air (Continental and Eastern) introduced MaxSavers in February, 1987, right after Continental incorporated People Express and New York Air. Fraught with unique and unprecedented restrictions, MaxSavers represented the most radical systemwide discount program ever offered by a U.S. airline. The public loved them and they were quickly copied by other airlines.

Continental/Eastern MaxSavers (and their equivalents) offer savings of up to 70 percent off unrestricted coach fares. MaxSaver fares range from $39 one-way (New York–Boston; Los Angeles–San Francisco) to $139 (New York–Seattle; Detroit–Los Angeles), $10 or so higher on Fridays and Sundays on some routes. Max-Savers are available on all Continental/Eastern routes; other carriers match them either systemwide or only where they compete with Continental or Eastern.

MaxSavers involve a unique array of restrictions:

- Two, seven, or 14-day advance purchase
- Round-trip travel, Saturday-night stayover
- Ticketing within 24 hours of making reservations
- Non-refundable: no cancellations or itinerary changes permitted
- Limited availability

Restrictions vary among carriers. Braniff permits a Friday- or Saturday-night stayover. On certain routes Pan Am requires neither advance purchase nor round-trip travel: These fares are, in effect, unrestricted, non-refundable fares available on a limited basis.

The *two, seven, or 14-day advance-purchase* requirement (depending on airline, season, and route) gives increased flexibility to both passenger and airline. Passengers can, theoretically at least, wait much longer to plan discount travel. (In practice, however, the most desirable MaxSaver seats are quickly snapped up.) And when an airline sees that it will have an excess of empty seats on a particular flight, it has time to transform those seats into MaxSavers.

The *24-hour ticketing* rule makes it more important than ever to cultivate a relationship with a travel agent. MaxSaver ticketing must be done in person, which means that within 24 hours of making a reservation you must appear at an airport, an airline in-town ticket office, or any travel agent. In most cases, a travel agent is the most convenient option.

The airlines really mean it about the *non-refundable* aspect of the ticket. If you change your plans or miss the plane, the airline owes you nothing. In some cases, airlines grant refunds when the passenger dies before departure and they occasionally allow passengers who produce medical certificates for serious illnesses or accidents to rebook. But they aren't obliged to do any of that and you certainly shouldn't count on it.

You can purchase insurance to cover potential loss on cancelled MaxSaver tickets. For $19 per person per ticket, the Travel Guard International Advance Purchase Plan trip cancellation policy will refund half of any penalty imposed (up to a maximum of $200) if you cancel for any reason. The policy will refund the full penalty for any cancellations due to certified emergencies. The policy also covers expenses incurred as a result of travel delay or baggage loss, collision damage on rental cars, and provides $25,000 worth of accidental death coverage. The policy must be purchased within two days of ticketing. Buy it from a travel agent or charge it by phone at 800-782-5151.

The most annoying MaxSaver restriction by far, however, is *limited availability*. Passengers calling for reservations frequently find that the flights of their desire are unavailable. This is particularly true for popular travel times on heavily-traveled routes. Continental and Eastern claim that about 40 percent of their total capacity is available for MaxSavers, but this doesn't mean 40 percent of every flight. Some flights may allot 80 percent of the seating to MaxSavers; others 20 percent; some have no MaxSavers at all.

The best advice for snagging MaxSaver-type fares is not to take "no" for an answer—at least don't take the first "no" for the final answer. When an airline reservationist tells you that no MaxSavers are available on a flight two weeks away, it almost always means that some seats are indeed available—but not at that price. They hope to sell those seats to someone else or to you either at a higher discount level or at unrestricted coach—five times the MaxSaver fare. If sales have not met expectations as flight time approaches, additional seats may become MaxSavers.

If you don't get your MaxSaver on your first call, ask to waitlist for it: Some airlines waitlist MaxSavers, some don't. But whether you're waitlisted or not, *keep calling back*. Make a special point of calling back for seven-day advance-purchase fares eight days before departure, the point where excess inventory frequently begets additional MaxSavers.

The *round-trip travel, Saturday-night stayover* requirement thwarts business travelers who usually don't stay over weekends. Even so, the extremely low fares sometimes make two MaxSavers cheaper than one unrestricted coach ticket. On the Chicago–New York (LaGuardia) route, United charges $238 roundtrip for MaxSavers and $620 roundtrip for unrestricted coach. The business traveler can buy a $238 MaxSaver with a departure from Chicago on Tuesday with a qualifying return; he or she then buys a separate $238 MaxSaver with a Wednesday departure from New York and another qualifying return. Assuming the loss of flexibility does not represent a problem, the business traveler has just saved $144!

What becomes of those unused return tickets—as well as other unwanted non-refundable tickets? Many are being sold through classified ads in daily newspapers, college papers, shoppers, etc. The Chicago *Sun-Times* lists such offerings under the heading of "Travel"; the San Francisco *Chronicle* under "Tickets for Sale or Wanted"; the Los Angeles *Times* under "Air Travel"; the Memphis *Commercial Appeal* under "Tickets (Sales, Exchange/Swaps)."

Since these tickets are officially non-transferable, it is illegal to sell, buy, or use them. In practice, however, airlines don't check IDs on domestic flights so you're not likely to be caught. (Don't buy someone else's ticket for foreign travel because the name on the ticket must match the name on a passport or other identification.) Be sure the name on the ticket has the same gender as your own and write out new luggage tags with the ticket-holder's name.

═══ TRADE-OFFS: ═══ MaxSavers	
Lowest fare available—up to 70 percent off normal coach	Round-trip travel and Saturday stayover required
Available systemwide on most airlines	Non-refundable tickets
Relatively short—2 to 14 days —advance-purchase requirement	Itinerary changes not permitted
	Tickets must be purchased *in person* within 24 hours of booking
	Limited availability; few seats or none available on some flights

Other Discount Programs

Beyond standard industry-wide MaxSavers, U.S. airfares become purely a matter of competitive caprice. With the demise of People Express and several other low-fare carriers, almost all airlines charge the same fares on similar routes—that is, they all have the same fare programs on the books and in the computer. What varies dramatically from airline to airline, day to day, hour to hour, and flight to flight is the *availability* of these fares.

To determine the most profitable proportion of seats at each discount level and at full fare, airlines practice the dark art of *yield management*. Yield management consists of computerized predictions of traffic on every particular flight. Predictions are based on past experience, industry trends, fare levels, and every other bit of relevant data the computer can digest. Initial seat allotments are formulated a year before departure but shift constantly in response to passenger behavior. The period of adjustment continues until a few hours before takeoff (up to 24 hours on some carriers), at which time only full-fare coach (Y) fares become available.

Given a hodgepodge of anonymous discount fares laden with business-traveler thwarting booking restrictions, finding the lowest fare becomes a matter of asking the right questions (see pp. 39–40) and weighing the importance of the following factors:

- *Discount levels* range from 20 and 70 percent off full-fare coach.

- *Advance-purchase periods* are either 30 days, 21 days, 14 days, 7 days, 3 days, 2 days, or 24 hours.
- *Ticketing deadline:* The length of time after you make a reservation in which you must purchase your ticket, ranges from 24 hours to 14 days.
- *Days of travel:* Best discounts are available on Tuesdays and Wednesdays, the lightest travel days; the fewest are offered on heavily-traveled Mondays and Fridays.
- *Departure times:* Best discounts are available for midday (11 A.M.–2 P.M.) and late-night (9 P.M.–6 A.M.) departures.
- *Flight itinerary:* Direct flights (one or more stops) and connecting flights (change of planes) often have better discounts than nonstops.
- *Cancellation penalties* range from 100 percent to zero depending on airline and particular discount-fare program.
- *Stayover requirement:* On domestic routes the discount fare requires a Saturday-night stayover or none at all. International travel often requires a seven-day minimum stay.
- *Roundtrip travel:* Most of the deeper discounts require round-trip travel.
- *Airports:* Better discounts may be available for flights into or out of particular airports in a metropolitan area.

APEX Fares

On international flights the principal permanent discount program is the old reliable APEX (Advance-Purchase Excursion) fare, the ancestor of the domestic Ultra-Saver. Round-trip APEX fares are available on most international routes, and the amount of the discount varies with the season. Some fares have three seasons—high, shoulder, and low—some two, and others never change.

At worst the round-trip APEX fare runs to about 60 percent of full-fare economy; at best it is less than half. APEX fares require a twenty-one–day advance purchase, round-trip travel, minimum stays of fourteen days, maximum stays of sixty days, and are subject to cancellation fees of varying amounts. Although heavily restricted, APEX fares are almost always the cheapest published international fares. (See "Bucket Shops" for unpublished fares.)

"Hopscotch" Fares

Generally speaking, Hopscotch fares exist for travel between major cities via a carrier that does not offer nonstop service between those cities. These fares are unrestricted but are available only on a limited-seating basis. Hopscotch fares—the label comes from Piedmont, which popularized the concept—are enticements for flights that include at least one stop, a plane change, or both.

Piedmont itself offers Hopscotch fares between northeastern cities such as New York, Boston, and Philadelphia, and western locales such as Chicago, Houston, Dallas, and New Orleans. Most flights require changes in Charlotte or some other southern city, but direct flights (one or more stops but no plane change) are available.

US Air also has a strain of Hopscotch-type fares on Pittsburgh connections between some of the major destinations it serves. The route map printed in the schedules for these airlines provides good clues to where Hopscotch fares may exist. Any two major cities on opposite sides of the airline's main hubs are plausible candidates.

Hopscotch fares are not the bargains they used to be. They are usually undercut by MaxSaver fares and by nonstop or direct service on cut-rate carriers flying those routes. However, these fares are sold on an unrestricted one-way basis if seats are available. So if you're too late to qualify for a MaxSaver and the cut-rate carriers are sold out, a Hopscotch fare may be the next best bet.

TRADE-OFFS: Hopscotch Fares	
Substantial savings over normal coach	Available on limited number of routings
No advance-purchase, round-trip travel, minimum/maximum-stay requirements	Stops and/or plane change required
	Increased travel time

"Hidden Cities"

Warning: Hidden-city (a.k.a. point beyond) ticketing is an explicit violation of airline tariff rules. Hidden-city tickets are also routinely written every day, often with the informed complicity of cooperative travel agents.

Hidden cities incorporate when competitive quirks in the airfare pricing systems often make it cheaper to buy a ticket to a point beyond a connection than to the connection point itself. To take advantage of this scam—and that's exactly what it is—you buy a ticket to the point beyond, either deplane or fail to board a connecting flight at the hidden city, and discard the coupon for the rest of the trip.

Until recently, Atlanta was the ultimate hidden city. A major hub for both Delta and Eastern, service into Atlanta itself was a closed shop with very high fares. But Atlanta was also the main connection point on the supercompetitive Northeast–Florida routes.

Passengers traveling from Philadelphia to Atlanta, for example, could buy a cheaper ticket from Philadelphia to Tampa, deplane in Atlanta, and discard the Atlanta–Tampa coupon.

The Hopscotch fares described in the previous section provide a promising area for rooting out hidden cities. I once paid $119 for a one-way Piedmont ticket from Newark to Chicago with a connection in Charlotte. On the first leg I sat next to a man who had paid $189 for his Newark–Charlotte ticket.

In this era of the hub-and-spoke, the hub itself is the most promising candidate for hidden-city status. Scrutinize airline schedules. If you're traveling to any hubs, check out whether it would be cheaper to be ticketed to a point beyond. The following is a list of the principal connecting hubs of the major U.S. airlines:

AIRLINE HUB CITIES

AMERICAN: Chicago, Dallas/Fort Worth, Nashville, Raleigh
CONTINENTAL: Houston (Intercontinental), Denver, Newark, Washington (Dulles)
DELTA: Atlanta, Dallas/Fort Worth, Cincinnati, Salt Lake City, Los Angeles
EASTERN: Miami, New York, Atlanta, Charlotte
NORTHWEST: Minneapolis, Seattle, Detroit, Memphis
PAN AM: New York, Los Angeles, Miami, Washington (Dulles)
PIEDMONT: Charlotte, Baltimore, Dayton
TWA: New York, St. Louis
UNITED: Chicago, Denver, Cleveland, San Francisco, Washington (Dulles)
US AIR: Pittsburgh

Hidden cities are worthwhile only as alternatives to full-fare coach. Cut-rate airlines and deep discount fares are usually cheaper. You cannot check baggage when flying to a hidden city because your suitcase will be checked through to the final destination.

Also, don't book a return trip on the same ticket as your hidden city. The airline might cancel the itinerary when you become a no-show on your first connecting flight.

⊕ TRADE-OFFS: ⊖
Hidden Cities

⊕	⊖
Savings over full-fare coach tickets on some routings	Extremely limited applicability
No restrictions	Violates airline tariff rules
Applicable for last-minute travel	No baggage check

Limited Service

Substantial savings are available on routes where airlines have service limited to only a few flights a day or week. Because these flights are scheduled to reposition aircraft rather than to compete with airlines flying full schedules on that route, they use low fares with no restrictions to fill up their planes.

Rooting out these limited-service bargains is a project for those who love to pore over airline schedules or the monthly *Official Airline Guide*, a listing of all flights in North America (all travel agents and some libraries receive it). I unearthed the $49 twice-a-week Pan Am flight from Seattle to San Francisco described in the introduction by scouring the Pan Am schedule.

During the periodic respites in the fare wars between the three airlines that offer virtually incessant service on the busy Los Angeles–San Francisco route—PSA, Air Cal, and United—cheap fares are still available for the limited service offered by the likes of Pan Am, TWA, Eastern, and Delta. Eastern has one flight a week each way between Chicago and New York (LaGuardia); this occurs only on Saturday and has fares as low as $64 one way.

To feed international flights leaving from New York (JFK), Pan Am and TWA offer limited service—one or two flights a day—to a number of non-coastal cities including Atlanta, Austin, Charlotte, Chicago, Cincinnati, Cleveland, Dallas, Detroit, Houston, Indianapolis, Louisville, Memphis, Nashville, Orlando, Philadelphia, Pittsburgh, Raleigh, and San Antonio. The fares on the legs to JFK are usually substantially lower than the unrestricted fares offered by other airlines on those routes. Travel agents can be a big help here: If a flight exists, their computers will list it.

⊕ TRADE-OFFS: Limited Service ⊖	
Low unrestricted fares	Few available and difficult to find
	Limited choice of flight days and times

Standby

As a cost-saving ploy, standby fares have virtually ceased to exist. Airlines prefer to award discounts to passengers who make their plans (and pay their money) far in advance rather than to those who risk waiting until the last minute. Although some carriers occasionally offer cut-rate standby specials, there are no regular low standby fares on any domestic route.

The only sources of standby savings are flights between many U.S. cities to London and occasionally other European destinations. These standby fares, however, are not available throughout the year but come and go with the changing of the seasons.

Standby is most likely to exist during peak seasons (May through October and around Christmas) when planes are normally filled than during off and shoulder seasons when there are fewer passengers. Airlines reason that passengers will expect to find available seats during slow seasons and thus avoid buying higher-priced coach tickets or APEX tickets in advance.

In recent years, the summer standby season lasted from April 1 to October 31. The one-way standby fare between New York and London has been $199 to $249; Chicago–London, $269 to $289; Los Angeles–London, $349 to $379. During standby periods, all airlines serving New York and London—Pan Am, TWA, British Airways (which also sells standby to Manchester), British Caledonian, Air India, El Al—charge the same fare. And with twelve to fifteen 747s taking off each day, the chances of finding a seat somewhere are pretty high. TWA has also offered standby fares ranging from $224 to $349 from all of its U.S. destinations to Amsterdam and Brussels.

The term "standby" is actually something of a misnomer, because you don't actually have to go to the airport hours before flight time and literally *stand by*. The term "same-day fare" is more accurate. On flight day, you can purchase a ticket and receive a confirmed reservation at an airline's in-town ticket office. From then on you're treated just like other economy-class passengers. If you can't make it to the ticket office or the airline won't confirm a seat, you can still head out to the airport and stand by.

⊕ TRADE-OFFS: ⊖
Standby

⊕	⊖
Lowest fare on major scheduled carrier to London and occasionally other European cities	Not available throughout year
	Uncertainty as to how, when, and whether you travel
Last-minute travel only	
Seats usually available	
Confirmed seating on day of purchase	

HOW TO FIND THE LOWEST AIRFARES

The U.S. airfare structure is in constant turbulence. All we can say with absolute certainty is that conditions will continue to change. It is possible, however, to find low fares by using certain procedures that work now, have worked in the immediate past, and, barring unforeseeable circumstances, will continue to work in the future.

"Never ask airline reservationists for a *coach*, *economy*, or *tourist* fare; instead request *the lowest available* one-way or round-trip fare."

● *When asking about airfares, always include the word "lowest" in your query.* Because the nomenclature of air travel is calculated to confuse, requesting "coach," "economy," "MaxSaver," "Super-Saver," "Ultra-Saver," or other budget fares can lead to all sorts of misunderstanding. Requests for "the lowest one-way fare" or "lowest round-trip fare" are impossible to misconstrue. Find out what the lowest fares are and work back from the restrictions.

If, for example, the lowest fare demands advance-purchase requirements that it is too late to satisfy, ask for a fare with briefer requirements. If a Saturday night stayover is unacceptable, ask for the next cheapest fare without that restriction. But in any case, begin at the bottom and work up to the most felicitous balance of price and pain.

● *Fares reflect peak flying times.* Lower fares—which may translate into a greater number of discount seats allotted to each flight—are usually available on Tuesday and Wednesday, Saturday, and sometimes Thursday. Friday, Sunday, and Monday are the most expensive days to fly. Lower fares may also be available on late-night (9 P.M.–6 A.M.) departures.

"Although no official "high," *shoulder* and *low* seasons exist in domestic air travel, the year's best fares are almost always offered throughout autumn and winter *except* during holiday weekends."

● *No official "high," "low," and "shoulder" seasons exist in domestic air travel, but airlines offer their most dramatic specials when business is slow.* The worst travel months for airlines (and the best for passengers) are mid-January through March and October through mid-December (except Thanksgiving weekend). Few specials are available during the summer, around Christmas, or during the Easter/Spring vacation.

● *Passengers can often save a lot by flying out of a "discount" airport in a nearby city.* Philadelphians, for example, can get much better fares from Newark. Other "expensive" cities that are reasonably close to discount cities are Milwaukee and Indianapolis (Chicago); San Diego (Los Angeles); and Richmond (Washington).

• *Be as flexible as possible about every aspect of ticketing.* Reservationists often access fare information on the basis of "time windows," the hours within which a passenger is willing to depart from one city or arrive at a destination. If you open your time window wider, more discount fares can fly through. Also make it clear that you are not averse to using any of the airports within a locality, take direct (one or more stops) flights, change planes, or suffer layovers—provided the airline makes it worth your while.

• *Recheck airfares once or even twice between the time you are ticketed and the time you fly.* If airlines lower the fare or introduce a new discount program after you are ticketed, they won't volunteer the refund. And once you fly, your chances of getting an adjustment are nil. The best times for rechecking both the airline you're on and its competition are a week after ticketing and a day or two before departure.

"Don't give up if airline reservationists tell you no more discount seats are available on particular flights: Cancellations and revised discount-seat allotments make it worthwhile to keep calling back."

• *Keep calling back to check on discount seats that have previously "shown out."* Cancellations and failure to meet ticketing requirements often result in previously unavailable seats being returned to the computer inventory. Good times for checking are thirty and fourteen days before departure when passengers who have not met advance-purchase requirements lose their reservations. Since the airlines input the new seats into the computers early in the day, that's the best time to call back.

• *Beware of misleading advertising.* The headline of a recent airline ad read: "Unrestricted Happiness. Every seat. Every day." The finer print below the price list stated that you had to travel round-trip and "buy your ticket at least seven days in advance." Where I come from, those constitute restrictions.

"Buy discount airfare tickets as soon as possible after making your reservation: If fares rise before you pay, you *are* subject to the increase."

• *If the airlines raise fares or alter conditions before you pay for the ticket, you have to pay the higher fares or meet the new conditions.* Fares constantly change without warning. If you've found a fare you can live with, purchase the ticket at once.

• The Department of Transportation (DOT) now handles consumer complaints concerning airlines. If you need assistance in a dispute or just want to put your complaint on record, call the Office of Community and Consumer Affairs at 202-755-2220 or write:

Office of Community and Consumer Affairs
U.S. Department of Transportation
400 7th Street, S.W.
Room 10405
Washington, DC 20590

A DOT pamphlet entitled *Fly Rights* contains a great deal of useful information about consumer-airline relations. Topics covered include airfares, delayed and canceled flights, overbooking, baggage, smoking, and safety. To receive a copy, send a check or money order for $1 payable to "Superintendent of Documents" and address to: Superintendent of Documents, Department 165-P, Consumer Information Center, Pueblo, CO 81009.

LOW-FARE CARRIERS

Before the Deregulation Act of 1978, the Civil Aeronautics Board strictly controlled domestic airline routings and fares. But deregulation changed everything. Suddenly existing airlines could fly wherever and whenever they wanted (within the United States) and charge any fare they chose. Similarly, new airlines could enter previously closed markets.

Since 1979, dozens of new airlines have been formed. Many of these were "paper airlines" that never got off the ground; some newcomers—Air Florida, Pride Air, Air One, World, and, most notably, People Express—have already been grounded. But the "upstart airlines" that have survived and flourished have permanently altered the character of the U.S. airline industry.

The Upstarts

Established airlines resent the newcomers, and it's easy to understand why. The old-timers had their fare levels protected, but they were required to provide full service on many unprofitable routes in return. Deregulation allows new airlines to come in and "skim the cream" with cut-rate service in the most lucrative markets.

New airlines ordinarily buy or lease used aircraft. And since new airlines are commonly nonunionized and have no high-salaried long-term employees, their labor costs are substantially below those of older carriers.

In terms of cost per passenger mile, the gauge of airline expenses, upstarts on average spend five and a half cents per mile while established carriers spend between seven and ten cents. Since the difference in per-mile cost derives mainly from differences in labor, the older airlines understandably think it's unfair that they should have to compete with rivals who play by a different set of rules.

The latest trend in deregulation is the onset of mega-airlines formed by mergers and takeovers: Texas Air now includes Continental, which incorporates People Express, Frontier, and New York Air plus full-fare Eastern; Northwest has taken over Republic; TWA incorporates Ozark; American includes Air Cal; and the USAir group consists of USAir, PSA, and Piedmont (pending).

Theoretically, these mergers could restore the stifling pre-deregulation conditions when a handful of large airlines flew everywhere and charged the same high fares. The difference today is that airlines are allowed to compete on the basis of price, and their cost structures require them to find ways to maximize passenger loads. It's true that regardless of how high fares rise, business people will have to fly and vacationers will jam every airport on Christmas Eve. But there aren't enough business travelers to fill every flight, and every night is not Christmas Eve. And if the upstart carriers and incessant fare wars have proven nothing else, they certainly have delineated a large market of travelers who will endure any ticketing restrictions thrown at them to obtain rock-bottom fares. Or they will stay home.

Throughout most of the year airlines need innovative fare programs to entice price-sensitive travelers onto their aircraft. And historically, the low-cost upstarts have come up with these programs. So even in this the darkening Age of the Mega-Airline, there is reason for low-fare hope.

LOW-FARE AIRLINES

The following section is a rundown of the most significant airlines that have gone into operation, adopted low-fare programs, or prospered since deregulation. If an airline has several toll-free numbers, the one listed here usually covers the largest area. If it doesn't work in your area, call toll-free information at 800-555-1212. If your area does not receive toll-free service, call local information.

America West

America West went into operation in 1983 and now serves forty-four cities in the United States and Canada. With Phoenix as its hub, the America West route map now extends northeast to New York (JFK), Baltimore, and Chicago; southeast to Austin and El

Paso; north to Edmonton and Calgary in Canada; northwest to Portland and Seattle; and west to Las Vegas and nine cities in California.

America West has business class, low unrestricted fares good on any flights, even lower fourteen-day, advance-purchase fares, and MaxSavers. Passengers get free drinks (including cocktails) and snacks on longer flights, oversize luggage bins and free baggage, newspapers, interline status for baggage and ticketing, and a frequent-flyer program. (800-247-5692, 5:00 A.M. to 1:00 A.M. Mountain Time only)

Braniff

After going temporarily out of business, Braniff was reborn as a low-fare carrier offering unrestricted and 7–30-day, advance-purchase fares to disparate destinations coast to coast. Passengers who cancel or change advance-purchase tickets can get either a 50 percent cash refund or 100 percent Braniff credit. Braniff serves New York (LaGuardia), Chicago, Detroit, Washington (Dulles and National), Boston, Miami, Phoenix, Las Vegas, San Antonio, Mexico City, San Diego, Seattle, San Francisco, Tucson, and Los Angeles but does not link all of those cities with one another. Braniff recently took over Florida Express, adding four Florida cities (Fort Lauderdale, West Palm Beach, Sarasota, Tampa), Nassau, and 11 destinations in the south and midwest to its system. Wednesday and Saturday travel is cheaper on some routes. Full in-flight service is standard. (800-BRANIFF)

Continental

On February 1, 1987, Texas Air Corporation, the parent company of Continental, acquired beleaguered People Express and merged it with Continental. Along with People Express (which itself had previously taken over Frontier, Britt, and PBA), Continental incorporated New York Air, another Texas Air subsidiary. Presidential Airways, a low-fare upstart headquartered at Washington (Dulles), then aligned itself with Texas Air as a Continental Express feeder. In 1986, Texas Air had acquired Eastern, a full-fare carrier which continues to operate separately.

All told, Texas Air has become the nation's largest air travel company. With nearly 20 percent of the total U.S. market and many overseas routes, it comprises the second-largest airline in the world: Only the Soviet Union's Aeroflot carries more passengers. Continental operates 1,500 daily flights to 140 destinations worldwide. It serves nearly every major U.S. city, Hawaii, western Canada, eight cities in Mexico, London, Paris, and has an extensive Asian/South Pacific operation.

A former full-fare carrier that emerged from Chapter 11 bankruptcy in 1983 as a non-unionized discounter, Continental has established a basic fare structure that is considerably lower than full-fare airlines. On the Boston–Los Angeles route, unrestricted coach—the highest coach fare—costs $330 one-way on Continental, $540 on United or American. Continental also offers a cut-rate first-class service, $450 one-way Boston–Los Angeles compared to $810 on the full-fares carriers.

As the largest airline, Continental is necessarily the largest low-fare airline and thus sets the pace for other carriers' discount programs. Continental had offered a typical array of 30-, 14-, and 7-day advance-purchase discounts, but in February, 1987, it stunned the public and the airline industry by introducing MaxSavers. Devised partly to publicize the Continental/People Express/New York Air merger and partly to camouflage a $10–$30 increase on all its unrestricted coach fares, MaxSavers were revolutionary in several important respects. They were the deepest discount ever, about 80 percent off unrestricted coach. They required round-trip travel and Saturday stayover, but demanded an unprecedentedly brief two-day advance purchase (since extended). Most importantly, MaxSaver tickets were non-refundable, a measure with which other airlines had experimented but never adopted system-wide. Other airlines quickly copied the popular MaxSaver program and are likely to continue to follow Continental's lead.

Unlike the late People Express, Continental is not a no-frills operation. Continental passengers receive complimentary soft drinks, meals, and baggage check. Continental assigns seats, has the TravelBank frequent flyer program, and offers first-class sections on each plane.

In other respects, however, Continental painfully recapitulates some aspects of the People Ex-perience. During the transitional post-merger period, Continental passengers suffered lengthy check-in lines and a dismaying amplitude of delayed and cancelled flights. Also the Newark Airport Zoo—locus of the most horrendous People Express nightmares, particularly on weekend evenings and holidays—lives, albeit shifted from decrepit North Terminal to Terminal B.

As discount avatar, Continental has come up with a wealth of innovative programs. Collegiate FlightBank, a frequent-flyer program for college students, awards full-time students between the ages of 16–25 airfare discounts and free trips for far fewer miles than the adult TravelBank. A membership costs $15 a year, $40 for four years.

For one lifetime membership fee of $25 ($75 with "companion privileges"), people over 65 can join the Golden Travelers Club and receive 10 percent discounts on Continental flights, automatic TravelBank membership, and hotel and car-rental discounts. In addition, Continental markets a Gold MasterCard linked to its TravelBank program. Every dollar charged to the card for any purchase becomes a credit for one mile in the TravelBank account. (Eastern has a similar program.)

Midway

Headquartered at Chicago Midway Airport, Midway Airlines beats the full-fare carriers on unrestricted Chicago connections between Atlanta, Boston, Detroit, New York (LaGuardia), Cincinnati, Des Moines, Denver, Cleveland, Dallas, Indianapolis, Washington (National), Minneapolis, Kansas City, Las Vegas, New Orleans, Omaha, Phoenix, and several destinations in Florida and the Caribbean. Uniquely, the Midway fourteen-day, advance-purchase round-trip fares have no Saturday-night stay requirement and a 50 percent cancellation penalty. Midway has full in-flight service and a frequent-flyer program. (800-621-5700)

Southwest Airlines

Because intrastate airfares were not regulated even before the Deregulation Act of 1978, Southwest Airlines prefigured the up-start no-frill revolution within the state of Texas. Southwest now offers unrestricted fares to twenty-seven cities in twelve states— including ten cities in Texas, Chicago (Midway), Detroit, St. Louis, New Orleans, Kansas City, Tulsa, Nashville, Little Rock, Las Vegas, Phoenix, Albuquerque, and four destinations in California.

Southwest has two fares on every routing: peak-time Executive Class fares on weekdays and Pleasure Class fares ranging from $15 to $20 less on weekends and after 7:00 P.M. on weekdays. It also offers lower Fun Fares that require 14-day advance purchase and are otherwise unrestricted; a youth fare that permits passengers twenty-one years old and under to pay Pleasure Class fares on any flight. No food is offered, but there are free soft drinks on all flights and free cocktails on Executive Class flights. After flying 20 one-way or ten roundtrip flights, passengers can become members of Southwest's frequent flyer program. (No toll-free number; in Dallas, call 817-640-1221.)

Virgin Atlantic

Virgin Atlantic offers 747 service from Newark and Miami to London (Gatwick) at unrestricted Economy fares of $349–$399 one way and advance-purchase fares of $239–$299 one way, depending on the season. Even cheaper non-refundable Late Savers may be booked within seven days of departure and Same Day Savers are available on day of departure. Virgin also has special children's fares and a children's section of the cabin.

Founded by Richard Branson, the owner of Virgin Records (Boy George and Culture Club), Virgin allows show-biz types to sing for their Super-Saver by entertaining on westbound flights during the winter. Virgin also offers Upper Class service for around $1,000 one way and low-cost connections to Maastricht, Holland. (800-862-8621)

ICELANDAIR FOREVER

Before Laker's Skytrain and well before Virgin Atlantic was even a twinkle in an investor's eye, Icelandair was offering low-fare scheduled service across the Atlantic. In 1953, an era when even charter flights were restricted to nominal members of affinity groups, Icelandair broke ranks with the other transatlantic airlines by offering fares about $300 below the competition. Icelandair started what the new low-fare upstarts later institutionalized: It made transatlantic travel an affordable reality for generations of middle-income tourists on both sides of the ocean.

Icelandair Today

Even in this era of low-fare airlines and cut-rate competition from the major carriers, Icelandair in some instances represents the best deal available. It essentially provides one-stop (at Reykjavík, Iceland) same-plane service between New York, Chicago, Baltimore, Boston, Orlando, and Luxembourg. (Flight frequency varies by season.) Luxembourg is a charming mouse-that-roared sort of country—bordering France, Germany, and Belgium—within a five-hour train trip of Amsterdam, Frankfurt, Paris, Brussels, and Geneva.

In addition to direct service, Icelandair offers through fares to its gateways from forty-eight U.S. cities using a number of U.S. carriers. It also offers Reykjavík connections to major Scandinavian cities and Luxembourg connections to major cities of Western Europe (Athens, Frankfurt, London, Paris, Rome, Zurich, among others).

Cut-rate Fare Programs

Super APEX

The fourteen-day advance-purchase, seven- to sixty-day stay Super APEX round trip undercuts similar fares offered by other transatlantic carriers. Depending on the season of travel, Super APEX between New York/Boston and Luxembourg ranges from

$399 to $599; from Chicago, $499 to $689; from Orlando, $499 to $699; from Baltimore, $429 to $629. Similarly priced through fares are available from fifty-one other U.S. cities. These fares are subject to a $75 cancellation fee.

Special Economy

While Super APEX fares compare favorably with other excursion fares, its unrestricted Special Economy fare represents even more dramatic savings. Whereas other carriers charge from $500 to $700 for one-way economy from New York to destinations on the continent, the comparable Icelandair fare from New York/Boston to Luxembourg is from $279 to $379 one way, and $479 to $679 round trip. The unrestricted New York–Frankfurt fare is from $489 to $689 round trip; New York–Paris, from $499 to $699. (Frankfurt and Paris service includes Reykjavik stops and Luxembourg connections.) Special Economy fares have no restrictions or cancellation fees.

Get Up And Go

To take advantage of Icelandair's version of standby, you must wait until within 48 hours of departure to make a reservation and buy a ticket. For a flight scheduled to depart at 7:45 P.M. on Friday, you can make a reservation any time after 7:45 P.M. on the preceding Wednesday and buy the ticket from Icelandair or a travel agent. The New York/Boston–Luxembourg Get Up and Go fare ranges from $149 to $199; from Baltimore, $159 to $209; from Chicago, $189 to $239; and from Orlando, $189 to $249.

Ground Connections

Well aware that few of its passengers have Luxembourg as a final destination, Icelandair offers free or low-cost ground transportation to and from Luxembourg. Passengers get free round-trip bus rides from the airport to several German cities—among them Frankfurt, Mannheim, Bitburg, Stuttgart, Düsseldorf, and Cologne; Liège, Belgium; and Amsterdam, Maastricht, Eindhoven, and Utrecht, Holland. Icelandair passengers are also entitled to discounted rail fares—$15 one way, $30 round trip—to any destination in Switzerland and some destinations in France (Paris $15/$30; Nancy/Strasbourg, $4/$8).

Icelandair Aircraft

The Icelandair experience has about it a charmingly nostalgic mood of discount travel past. This might have something to do

LOW-FARE CARRIERS

RT = Discounts for round-trip travel; AP = Deeper discounts for advance purchase; FF = Operates frequent-flyer program

AIRLINE	PHONE #	RT	AP	FF	REMARKS
America West	800-247-5692	Yes	7–14 days	Yes	Serves 44 cities in the Midwest, Northeast, Far West, and Western Canada from Phoenix hub
Braniff	800-BRANIFF	Yes	30 days 7 days	No	Operates coast to coast from hubs in Kansas City, Orlando, and Dallas/Fort Worth; lower fares available Tues., Wed., Sat. on some routes
Continental	800-525-0280	Yes	7–30 days	Yes	Low unrestricted fares and a range of discounts to most U.S. destinations through Denver, Newark, and Houston hubs; also flies to Mexico, London, and the Pacific.
Midway	800-621-5700	Yes	14 days	Yes	Service from Chicago (Midway) hub to major cities of Northeast, Midwest, Florida, Las Vegas, and the Caribbean
Southwest Airlines	No toll-free number. In Dallas, call: 817-640-1221.	No	14 days	No	Peak/off-peak service to 25 cities in Midwest, Southwest, and Far West; youth fares; no food but free soft drinks on all flights
Virgin Atlantic	800-862-8621	No	21 days	No	Unrestricted and advance purchase fares to London (Gatwick) from Newark and Miami; cancellation penalties; lower Late Saver and Same Day fares available; upper-class premium service

with the equipment—narrow-bodied DC-8s that, along with the Boeing 707, made up the first generation of transatlantic jets. Nostalgia, however, does not necessarily bespeak comfort.

Icelandair's DC-8s are crowded. With a 249-passenger single-class six-across seating, seats are configured so tightly that windows are not always aligned with rows. (By contrast, the DC-8s flown by United, one of the last U.S. airlines to fly them, have more than fifty fewer seats.) Legroom and overhead storage space is minimal, and passengers should avoid carrying on anything that further constricts the scant opening beneath the seat in front of them.

In addition, the antique planes are beginning to show their age, their seat covers worn thin by generations of bargain hunters. They lack audio or video in-flight entertainment, but meals are ample and good—you get two with free wine on transatlantic trips—and the service is briskly courteous.

Transit Stop

The mandatory transit stop at Reykjavík's Keflavik airports hearkens to the era when planes couldn't make it all the way "across the pond" without refueling. Located three hours from Luxembourg and six to seven hours from Icelandair's North American destinations, the Reykjavík transit stop is a welcome break during which passengers must deplane and spend an hour or so in the airport.

The Keflavik terminal houses two stores. The duty-free shop purveys the usual duty-free bounty—liquor, tobacco, chocolate, perfumes, and electronics—at not particularly tempting prices. The duty-free shops at the Luxembourg Airport have better deals.

The Icemart stocks a wide selection of all-Icelandic goods— woolens, furs, books, caviar, cheeses. Prices seem steep, but how often do you have a chance to buy anything indigenously Icelandic?

Icelandair also markets a number of low-cost Iceland stopover package tours.

Luxembourg

The city of Luxembourg is a charming medieval city that blends the French, Belgian, and German cultures. If you arrive the night before departure, you can spend the night in one of the many inexpensive hotels located near the railroad station. In the morning, take a tour of the city (it leaves from the station and includes a stop at General Patton's grave in the American cemetery). Buses to Luxembourg Airport also depart from the railroad station.

Moderate Savings, Moderate Discomfort

Icelandair falls into the moderate-savings, moderate-discomfort category and offers low fares on a reliable scheduled carrier airline to a central European destination. For those who don't have time to comply with the advance-purchase requirements of other airlines, Icelandair can represent considerable savings. And the adventurous will enjoy the opportunity to visit, even briefly, such little-known nations as Iceland and Luxembourg.

Nostalgia notwithstanding, Icelandair is definitely a few-frills operation—crowded planes, scant amenities—and travel takes much longer than for normal nonstops. Between the five-hour forty-five–minute leg from New York to Iceland, the one-hour transit stop, and the three-hour leg from Iceland to Luxembourg, a trip to Europe takes nearly ten hours on Icelandair. By contrast, a nonstop flight from New York to Frankfurt (the nearest nonstop destination) takes only seven hours and fifteen minutes. (Toll-free number: 800-223-5500)

TRADE-OFFS: Icelandair	
Low fares from five U.S. gateways to convenient European destinations	Longer travel times—three hours longer than nonstops
Low joint fares to Luxembourg from fifty-one U.S. cities	Crowded cabins
	No in-flight entertainment
Great for last-minute travel with Special Economy or Same-Day reservations	Less than daily service from every U.S. gateway except New York
Cheap or free bus or rail connections to Germany, Belgium, Holland, and France	
Reykjavík transit stop	
Luxembourg	
Nostalgia factor	

LOWEST-FARE SPECIALISTS

Domestic airfares are just too complex for the human mind to comprehend. On every routing, dozens of airlines—established carriers and upstarts alike—offer a vast selection of fares laden with Byzantine conditions for purchasing what are essentially identical products. And along with presenting a multitude of options, airfares are also extremely "perishable"—subject to alteration or complete disappearance. An estimated 76,000 fares change *every day*.

Even if you're traveling within a reasonably rigid time frame point to point between two cities, lowest-fare specialists can sniff out fares that would elude both passengers and the most well-equipped, competent travel agents. These specialists are particularly valuable when you add extra stops or fly to one city and return from another or have any other kind of complication in your itinerary.

Fairest of the Fares

Guaranteed lowest fares are available from independent agencies or from local branches of national travel agencies that have created their own lowest-fare computer programs. What do these agencies possess that the Mom-and-Pop travel agency on the corner lacks? Access to most or all of the computerized reservation systems operated by the airlines; electronic access to the Airline Tariff Publishing Company in Washington (the official repository of all airline fares); and employees who spend all of their time processing this avalanche of information to "creatively construct" the lowest fares on any desired routing.

"Lowest fare," in this context, is not necessarily synonymous with "poorest service," "least convenience," or "fewest frills." The lowest fare on a particular routing may involve a nonstop flight on a major airline at the busiest time of day. It may also involve red-eye flights, secondary airports, plane changes at unexpected locales, multistop flights, and layovers. Sometimes the hassles make the savings more trouble than they're worth; often there are no hassles at all.

Traveltron

Traveltron, an Irvine, California, firm that has been creatively constructing low fares since 1983, compares the difference between themselves and regular travel agents to the difference between general practitioners and brain surgeons. "A travel agent has to know about airfares plus cruises, tours, hotels, car rentals, visas, everything," says assistant vice-president Linda Honsa. "All our people do all day every day is put together airfares."

Traveltron uses the computerized reservation systems of several competing airlines to eliminate computer bias. Although every system lists all of the flights on a particular route, the "host" airline that markets the program lists its own flights and those of paying guests, or "co-hosts," in the most favorable positions. Host and co-host flights appear prominently on the top lines of the first computerized "pages" for each routing. By accessing and comparing the number of competing computer systems, low-fare specialists are able to counteract the bias inherent in any single system.

In the process of using several computerized reservation systems to eliminate bias, low-fare specialists also ensure last-seat availability. Last-seat availability becomes an asset because the reservation systems of host airlines allot a specified number of seats on their own flights to systems operated by rival carriers and withhold the rest for their own clients. A TWA flight, for example, might show "out" on the American Sabre System computers while TWA's own PARS system still indicates that seats are available. With access to all of the computer systems, Traveltron can offer last-seat availability on any flight.

Tricks of the Trade

Beyond the standard practices, Traveltron uses a variety of abstruse methods to construct the lowest fares. It may be a matter of finding a *hub city* where you can make the best connection or of using a *hidden city*. They may be able to locate *joint-fare* arrangements between major airlines and commuter carriers or write *open-jaw* tickets that allow you to save by returning (or in some instances not returning) from a city other than the one into which you flew.

Combined fares involve ticketing on different airlines for the same trip. For instance, Traveltron recently found that on a given day, the best round-trip fare between Los Angeles and Pittsburgh could be obtained by making a connection in Albuquerque! Traveltron keeps track of all *introductory* and *promotional* fares, and it knows when these are going to change.

The Traveltron national reservation line is 714-851-8073, and it operates Monday through Friday between 6:00 A.M. and 6:00 P.M. Pacific time. If you buy a ticket from them, they will reimburse you for the call after you submit copies of your phone bill and itinerary. Traveltron prefers to charge travel to major credit cards but also accepts cashier's checks.

Traveltron delivers tickets—including boarding passes—through the mail if there is sufficient time. If the time factor precludes this courtesy, they get a favorable price on delivery by Federal Express (which the customer pays) that is less than $10 for next-day delivery and even less for day-after-next service. They can also arrange prepaid tickets at the airport, but this costs more than Federal Express ($10) and may involve waiting in line. For cancellations or changes in itineraries, Traveltron operates a Preferred Customer Line.

Other Farebusters

Fare Finders in Beverly Hills uses a methodology similar to Traveltron's to unearth the lowest fares on any routing. They deliver tickets by mail within five to ten working days or arrange for prepaid ticketing. They can be reached at 213-652-6303 Monday through Friday from 9:00 A.M. to 6:00 P.M. Pacific time.

Ask Mr. Foster travel agencies have access to a staff of fare specialists who review fares twenty-four hours a day. Thomas Cook Travel guarantees "the lowest airfare at the time of ticketing," but only to corporate clients. American Express agencies can also access lowest-fare computer programs.

TRADE-OFFS:
 Lowest-Fare Specialists ⊖

⊕	⊖
Lowest scheduled fares on any domestic routing	May have to "earn" lowest fares with:
Applicable for both advance-purchase and last-minute travel	• multiple stops • plane change • layovers
Particularly valuable for itineraries with two or more stops	• off-hours flights • inconvenient airports • any or all of the above
Often arranges nonstop service on full-frills carriers	
Last-seat availability	

CHARTER FLIGHTS

Like other segments of the travel industry, the charter-flight business has changed drastically in recent years. Charters used to be limited to members of affinity groups. If you weren't already a card-carrying member of, say, the Oregon Geography Teachers Association or the Left-Handed Atheists Club, you had to arrange for nominal membership, fly over with the group, and reconvene for the return flight. Purchase of a ground package—hotels, meals, tours—was often a prerequisite to taking advantage of the charter fare.

In 1978, the Civil Aeronautics Board opened charters to the public and permitted a great deal more flexibility and competitiveness than had previously existed. Now anyone can fly a public charter. You can make air-fare only arrangements, and need no longer adhere to the schedule of any group. You can fly charters into one city and return from somewhere else. You can even buy one-way tickets, known in charter-industry lingo as "half round trips."

Wholesale Tour Operators

The principal difference between chartered and scheduled flights is that with charters you deal directly not with airlines but with entities known as *wholesale tour operators*. Tour operators charter entire planes or segments of planes from airlines to fly specific routes at specific times. They set fares and sell tickets either through their own retail outlets, through travel agents (the most common form of distribution), or through "off-price" dealerships (see headings for "Standby Brokers," and "Last-Minute Travel Clubs," in index). Tour operators also provide (or choose not to provide) preflight and in-flight services.

Charter Airlines

Charter flights may take place on regularly scheduled airlines: Pan Am, United, TWA, and British Airways all handle a considerable amount of charter business. More commonly, tour operators use airlines such as Martinair, Condor, Tower Air, Spantax, Balair, LTU, American Trans Air, and Rich International—carriers that principally handle charters. (Free-lance writer Judith Stone insists that she once took a charter flight on a generic airline that flew a plain-white craft with the word "Airplane" stenciled along the side.)

Charter Advantages

The main advantage of charter flights is price. Although fares fluctuate considerably between and within seasons, charters usually cost from $50 to $100 less than the lowest round-trip excursion fare (APEX or Super APEX) on a scheduled airline from the East Coast to Europe, and from $100 to $200 less than scheduled flights from the West Coast. Geared to day-by-day changes in travel patterns, charter fares run slightly lower on off-days and slightly higher on holiday weekends.

Larger tour operators with many flights to different places sell *half round trips* (one-way tickets) that permit you to fly to one destination and return from another. Two half round trips cost only slightly more than one "whole" round trip. Other large operators even allow some flexibility for altering your return trip, although this privilege cannot be counted upon on every charter.

Charters often provide the *only nonstop or direct service overseas from interior cities*. Direct service from Salt Lake City to Frankfurt or New Orleans to Paris is simply unavailable on scheduled carriers.

Charters within Europe play a substantially greater role in the cut-rate air transportation scene. The European air transportation industry is a highly *un*-deregulated mechanism where prolific discounting simply does not exist. Because charters often represent the only alternative to the full economy fare, they are often the cheapest and most convenient way to travel within Europe.

Charter Drawbacks

Along with the many pluses, charters also have serious drawbacks, some of which can be overcome by smart shopping, while others are subject to the luck of the draw.

Charters don't go everywhere. While many charter flights take off for Paris, London, and Rome, few are available to countries whose governments have protectionist policies toward national or state-owned airlines. Consequently, few charters are available to Scandinavia or the Far East.

Charters are seasonal. Plenty of flights head east (toward Europe) in the summer and south (toward the Caribbean) in the winter, but there are very few the other way around.

Charters have limited and inflexible schedules. Tour operators typically arrange back-to-back-flights on which planes fly from, say, Denver to Florence on Friday night and return from Florence to Denver on Saturday morning. You can stay any number of weeks, but you cannot fly within the week or on any other day.

Charter passengers must pay for the charter flight weeks and possibly months in advance. Tour operators will sell seats until the last minute, but in practice the most desirable dates fill up early. Also, passengers who alter or cancel their travel plans are subject to substantial penalties.

Rights of Passage

Despite the drawbacks described above, charter passengers are not completely unprotected. If the tour operator cancels the trip ten days or more before the departure date, passengers must be notified in writing and receive a refund within fourteen days. Similarly, if a major change is made more than ten days before departure—an increase in the fare that exceeds 10 percent, change in the itinerary—passengers have seven days in which to cancel, and the operator has fourteen days in which to send a full refund. Tour operators can't raise fares within ten days of departure, but they are allowed to reschedule flight times by as much as forty-eight hours without penalty.

The Charter Experience

In and of itself, the charter-flight experience has caused many an otherwise intrepid traveler to vow "never again."

• *Long lines* Whereas passengers on scheduled international flights are usually asked to check in an hour prior to departure, charter passengers generally must arrive three to four hours early. Most of the additional time is spent standing with luggage in lengthy understaffed check-in lines.

• *Crowded cabins* While some tour operators charter the regular aircraft of scheduled airlines (or, on occasion, buy space on scheduled flights), most flights take place on specially configured charter aircraft. The most comfortable charter planes are wide-body Boeing 747s, which usually have ten-across seating with a pitch (distance between rows) of thirty-two to thirty-four inches. Narrow-body 707s and DC-8s, first-generation transatlantic jets now banished from some airports by antinoise regulations, have six-across seating but less pitch (read less legroom) than scheduled carriers.

The worst charter planes in the sky are certain specially configured DC-10s and L-1011s with ten-across narrow seats and a pitch of only thirty-one to thirty-two inches. When seating capacity on a DC-10 or L-1011 exceeds 370 seats, get ready for a tight squeeze.

• *Meager in-flight amenities* In-flight services—movies, food, drinks—are supplied by the tour operator. Since economy is the predominating principal, don't expect much. On boarding an Air France charter from New York to Paris, a couple was pleasantly surprised to receive two packages—a "Welcome Aboard" present, they imagined, a vial of cologne, perhaps a beret. They were less pleasantly surprised to find that the parcels represented the entirety of in-flight service: box-lunch supper and breakfast.

• *Late departures* Charter flights are notoriously late, often by hours and not infrequently by days. Most charter airlines have a limited inventory of aircraft. As a result, if one plane is delayed by mechanical difficulty, you have to wait until it's fixed. Unless the flight is delayed by more than forty-eight hours, federal law mandates no form of compensation.

• *Safety* Charter airlines may adhere to less stringent safety procedures than do scheduled airlines. This situation was brought tragically to light in December 1985, when the crash of a DC-8 chartered from Arrow Air killed 248 U.S. servicemen and 8 crew members.

Fear of Failure

There is a real possibility that the charter airline or tour operator will declare bankruptcy before or during your trip. It happens almost every year. Airline failure is less common and less disastrous. The tour operator probably still has the money passengers paid (he or she is obliged to keep it in an escrow account until the flight) and can make arrangements with another airline. A failure that occurs during a trip might necessitate a few days' delay while alternative arrangements are made, but it probably won't cost additional money.

Tour-operator failure is more common and more serious. Tour operators are required to post performance bonds and place payments for flights in escrow accounts earmarked for air travel. If the operator fails before you depart, you should be able to get your money back. This is hardly an ironclad guarantee, because the performance bond seldom covers the entire cost of chartering the aircraft.

If the tour operator fails during your trip, you may be at least temporarily stranded. In a worst-case scenario, the charter airline refuses to carry you because the tour operator hasn't paid them. No other charter or scheduled carrier is obligated to honor the ticket or has anything to gain by doing so. You are then faced with a delay of perhaps several days, the increased expense of obtaining another ticket, and little likelihood of ever receiving a full refund. Eventually the tour operator or airline may rescue you with some alternative arrangement. But this could take several days and if you're in a hurry to get back, you may have to pay the price.

If you have qualms about a tour operator's reliability or solvency, contact your local Better Business Bureau. To find out whether any enforcement complaints have been lodged against a tour operator or charter airline, contact the Department of Transportation in Washington, D.C., at 202-755-2220.

━━━━━━━━━━◆TRAVELER'S ALERT◆━━━━━━━━━━

Whenever possible, pay for charter flights with charge cards. In case of problems later, you can withhold payment or try to get a refund through the charge-card company.

If you can't put it on plastic, make sure your check is made out to the escrow or trust account U.S. operators are legally required to establish for each charter program. If you make the check payable to the individual tour operator, you diminish your chances of receiving a refund in case of failure.

To protect yourself against airline or operator failure, you can buy "travel protection" or "trip interruption" insurance from a travel agent or tour operator. Insurance costs around $5 per $100 of protection, but some travel agencies offer it as a free perk for buying through them.

In any event, when flying a charter be sure to have the financial wherewithal—charge card, traveler's check, cash—to buy your way home in an emergency.

Choosing a Charter

Travel agents receive listings of all charter flights and can book space on any of them. But charters are not a travel agency's favorite kind of business. Because fares are lower, commissions are lower. Charter flights are not computerized, so agents must check them out through brochures and book them over the phone. Since agents must work harder to make less money booking a charter, they tend to be relatively uninformed and negative about them.

If you decide to fly a charter, your best bet is to track it down yourself and have an agent write the ticket. This is more than merely convenient. In some cases of failures by charter carriers or tour operators, tickets purchased through accredited agencies have received priority refunds.

Charters advertise widely during the months preceding flights. Check out local newspapers and the Sunday travel section of the paper in your most convenient gateway city—the *New York Times*, *Boston Globe*, *Miami Herald*, *Chicago Tribune*, *Los Angeles Times*, *San Francisco Chronicle*, and others. The *Village Voice* also lists numerous charter flights, most of which depart from New York.

You can also contact charter companies directly. Some of the oldest and most reputable firms include Council Charter (800-223-7402; 212-661-0311), a thirty-nine-year-old subsidiary of the private not-for-profit Council on International Educational Exchange, whose charter flights are available to everyone; Travac (800-872-8800; 212-563-3303), a specialist in European charters; and Unitravel (800-325-2222; 314-727-8888), which offers "half round trips" between sixteen U.S. cities (among them St. Louis, Minneapolis, Detroit, Cleveland, and Houston), and nine cities in Europe.

Charter flights are not our favorite mode of cheap/smart travel. They must be arranged far in advance and their itineraries are relatively inflexible. And while the risk of a failure that leaves you stranded in Transylvania is slight, so too may be the price differential between the charter and the best advance-purchase excursion fares. Unless the charter offers truly dramatic advantages in terms of cost and convenience—and from some destinations on some charters this may well be the case—the greater security, comfort, and flexibility offered by a scheduled service is usually worth the extra money.

	TRADE-OFFS: Charter Flights	⊖
Low fares—from $50 to $100 less than lowest discount fares from East Coast to Europe, from $100 to $200 less than fares for West Coast One-way and round-trip fares available Fly into one city, return from another Last-minute travel possible	Inflexible itinerary Limited choice of destinations and flight times Potential flight delays Crowded aircraft Few-frills in-flight service possible Penalty for cancellation and changes	

STANDBY BROKERS

Remember student standby? This splendid program dates back to 1966, when American Airlines and eventually the other major carriers began selling students (actually anyone between the ages of twelve and twenty-two) I.D. cards for $3 permitting them to fly standby anywhere the airline went for half of the regular fare.

Almost overnight, student standby transmogrified the demographics of the U.S. air-travel industry. Suddenly airplane cabins, heretofore the near exclusive preserve of businessmen (yes, *men*) in suits, were crammed with a motley array of student bodies newly upgraded from their accustomed trains and buses. Student standby introduced the monstrous population cohort of early baby-boomers to the wonders of flying—and they saw that it was good. Student standby got an entire generation of affluent potential customers hooked on air travel.

Today the cheap standby fare is virtually nonexistent. Airlines prefer to award low fares to passengers who make plans (and turn over their cash) far in advance. Except for the standby tickets available intermittently throughout the year between various U.S. cities and London, standby means only "no reservation," not "lower fare."

Although you can't save on standby tickets from the airlines themselves, a new breed of middleperson now markets standby seats for international charter and scheduled flights. Functioning as last-minute clearinghouses for distressed merchandise, these dealers can get you overseas for considerably less than what you would pay charter operators or airlines for identical service.

Airhitch

The oldest established standby broker, Airhitch (2901 Broadway, Suite 100, New York, NY 10025; 800-372-1234; 212-864-2000), openly promises to get you to Europe at the least possible cost. What it doesn't stipulate is exactly where in Europe or precisely when you can expect to arrive.

"(Airhitch) is ideally suited to free-spirited people wishing to get across the North Atlantic at the lowest possible cost, who do not have rigorous preferences as to destination or departure date," reads an Airhitch brochure. "It can also be used to great advantage by persons who may have a specific destination in mind, as long as they understand the basic limitations of the service. It should definitely *not* be used by persons who have more money than time, or who have a lot of baggage, or who cannot live with last-minute deviations from expected itineraries."

Airhitch fares are amazingly low—$160 one way from East Coast gateways (usually New York, sometimes Boston, Baltimore, Philadelphia, or Washington; occasionally Atlanta or Miami); $229 from the Midwest; and $269 from the West Coast. In 1986, Airhitch boarded passengers in sixteen U.S. gateways.

And while destinations may be "any major jet airport in Western Europe," about 90 percent of the flights land within a 300-mile radius of Brussels, a circle that encompasses Paris, London, Amsterdam, and Frankfurt.

Airhitch Procedure

To sign up for Airhitch, you must first fill out a "space-available registration form and receipt voucher." To establish the "date range" within which you can fly, you list "earliest possible departure date," "preferred departure date," and "latest departure date." You also list a preferred destination, plus second and third choices. The minimum date range is five days, but what is the optimum date range? "In this case the optimum is the maximum," says Airhitch founder Robert Segelbaum. "If you don't care when you go, the probability of getting a flight is virtually 100 percent."

When you've returned the registration form with a $25 deposit, Airhitch will mail back a stamped receipt/voucher. Three days before the beginning of your date range, you begin calling a toll-free number to find out what "flight opportunities"—most likely departure cities, destinations, dates, and boarding possibilities—are available during your date range.

You indicate which flight you prefer and arrange to deliver or send the balance due ($135 from the East Coast; $204 from the Midwest; $244 from the West Coast) to the Airhitch New York office or to a local Airhitch coordinator (Airhitch accepts traveler's checks, cashier's checks, and cash). You will then receive a validated voucher and instructions for meeting at the airport the person authorized to get you on the plane.

Since Airhitch deals in merchandise it doesn't receive until the last minute, it proffers no ironclad guarantees. It does claim that 99 percent of its customers fly during their date range and 95 percent fly on the first flight to which they have been assigned. Airhitch also has provisions for altering the date range, specifying destinations, and making alternative arrangements if you miss an appointed flight.

Along with the New York home office, Airhitch has local coordinators in Los Angeles, Washington, D.C., Miami, Chicago, and Albuquerque. Airhitch can arrange return trips from Europe for similar fares. You can register with them before you leave the states or at their year-round offices in London and Hamburg.

Low-Cost Confirmations

Airhitch can also book confirmed seats on charter or scheduled flights at slightly higher fares. Airhitch Target Flights consists of confirmed seats from specific cities to specific destinations at a specific price on or about a specific date. This is accomplished by targeting those four factors and "checking the air transportation marketplace for the best available deals." Airhitch claims a 95 percent success rate in hitting the target precisely and that the remaining 5 percent deviate by only one of the four factors (date, departure city, destination, or fare).

While target fares are priced individually according to flight date and carrier, figure on paying from $180 to $200 one way for travel between New York and major destinations such as Paris, London, Amsterdam, and Frankfurt; and from $350 to $380 for round trip; for other cities in Europe (Munich, Shannon, Vienna, Madrid, Rome, Athens, and others), the fare ranges from $260 to $320 one way and $420 to $600 round trip.

To arrange a Target Flight you must obtain a Service Request asking for preferred departure dates, departure city, destination, and return date, if any. If you book less than forty-five days prior to departure, you must submit the form with full payment; only a 50 percent deposit is required if you book further ahead.

A few days prior to your departure date, you must call the office to find out your departure time and itinerary. Ideally, the arrangements will not change after that; less ideally, you will not know your itinerary until the day before you fly. If Target Flight can't get you exactly what you want, it will search for acceptable alternatives. Even if you refuse what it offers you, the company will retain a service fee of $25 and refund the remainder as a credit toward future services.

 ⊕	**TRADE-OFFS:** **Standby Brokers**	 ⊖
Lowest fares available to many European destinations Excellent for last-minute travel decisions Possibility of flying full-frill carriers		Standby situation— uncertainty as to flight time, destination, and whether travel will occur Possibility of flying few-frills, overcrowded charter flights Complicated ticketing procedure No charge-card acceptance

OFF-PRICE TRAVEL DEALERS: AMERICA'S BUCKET SHOPS

The term "bucket shop" is thought to have originated in Boston, where dealers bought blocks of stock in companies and divided them into smaller units for smaller investors. In travel marketing terms, bucket shops are travel companies that sell "off-price" tickets to the public. The airlines give them blocks of tickets they don't expect to sell at the published fare but prefer not to sell at a discount themselves or through "straight" travel agencies.

The airlines aren't fond of these operations, but they use them. As far as the passenger is concerned, flying on off-price tickets is entirely legitimate.

American Bucket Shops

Off-price travel services sell unofficially discounted tickets to virtually all overseas destinations. (They do not, at this time, handle domestic service.) Although these outlets might come up with tickets on almost any carrier at one time or another, much of the inventory comes from foreign-flag carriers on flights to destinations not located within the national homeland.

For example, Pakistan Airlines distributes many of the seats on two weekly flights between New York and Paris through off-price outlets. Kuwait Airways' New York–London tickets are also frequently available. Off-price dealers often sell overstock of major international carriers.

The Price Is Right . . .

The big advantages of off-price dealers are low prices and few restrictions. These outlets sell relatively unrestricted round-trip tickets to European destinations for around $200 less than the lowest APEX fares. *As a rule, off-price tickets get you about 60 percent off the normal unrestricted economy fare and 30 percent off APEX fares.*

These fares carry fewer restrictions than do APEX fares, the principal international discount fare program. Whereas APEX fares require advance booking and purchase, minimum stays, and maximum stays, off-price fares seldom have advance-purchase requirements, require stays of only a day or so, and have maximum stay periods ranging from several months to a year.

Keep in mind that this usually involves regularly scheduled flights on major international carriers. You receive meals, beverages, free baggage check, and all of the other amenities of economy class. (Bucket shops may also ticket charter flights.)

. . . But Flexibility Is Limited

The disadvantages come into play if you alter your plans. Because of the way tickets are distributed, you must get a refund from the agency at which you buy your ticket; this usually entails a substantial penalty. Unlike regular full-fare and some discount tickets, you can use these tickets only on the airline that issued them. Also, you have no flexibility in changing an itinerary in the middle of a trip.

Off-price dealers are particularly useful when you must travel on short notice. Recently, when I needed to get to London right away, the only remaining low-fare carrier on the route, Virgin Atlantic, was already booked and standby tickets on the major airlines (Pan Am, TWA, British Airways, British Caledonian) were not available at that time of the year. A desperate survey of New York off-price travel dealers unearthed a number of intriguing alternatives.

Every dealer wanted to sell me a ticket on a Tuesday or Saturday night Kuwait Airlines flight. Although the published price for a one-way economy ticket from Kuwait itself was $388, various bucketeers quoted rates of $175 on Tuesday, $203 on Saturday; $199 plus $6 if I used a credit card; $189 plus a $3 service charge on Tuesday, and $229 plus $7 on Saturday; $210; and $259—all for the same seat on the same plane.

My search also turned up a cut-rate seat on a Saturday night Pan Am flight. I could have paid $180 to fly as a courier (with baggage restrictions and other responsibilities, see index under "Courier Services") or $189 plus a $15 service charge to fly "normally."

These outfits keep a selection of discount irons in the fire. If you are somewhat flexible, you are certain to score some sort of deal—but don't buy the first thing you see.

Finding Off-Price Dealers

The easiest way to find domestic bucket shops is through ads in local newspapers. Try the Sunday travel section or check out classified ads under the "Travel" or "Tickets" headings.

Barring that, the Sunday travel sections of the *New York Times, Los Angeles Times, San Francisco Examiner, Chicago Tribune,* and most other major dailies normally include ads from a dozen or so off-price dealers. They are usually one- or two-column–inch boxes that include a laundry list of fares, an address, and a phone number, but not much else. The *Village Voice* runs a number of similar ads and *USA Today* usually has a few ads for off-price dealers in its "Discount Travel" classifieds. Please note that the price you see in these ads is seldom the price you ultimately pay—the term "bait and switch" comes to mind. Advertised fares are frequently unavailable, and you usually wind up paying somewhat more.

One reputable off-price dealer is Nouvelles Frontiers, which has offices in New York (19 W. 44th Street, New York, NY 10036; 212-764-6494), San Francisco (209 Post Street, San Francisco, CA 94108; 415-781-4480), and Los Angeles (6363 Wilshire Blvd., Los Angeles, CA 90048; 213-658-8955). Access International (250 W. 57th St., Suite 511, New York, NY 10107; 800-548-4881; 212-333-7280) also markets bucket-shop tickets from 34 cities.

Keep in mind that most flights on bucket-shop tickets depart only from major gateways, usually New York. Some may be able to arrange discount transportation to the gateway; otherwise you will have to get there on your own.

To accommodate travelers who use New York as a transit stop for overseas travel, the Port Authority of New York & New Jersey publishes a 36-page brochure listing sixteen en route vacation packages. To receive a free copy of *On-Your-Way-Over Stopovers,* call 800-782-6837 (in NY, 212-688-7741), or write: The Port Authority of NY & NJ, On-Your-Way-Over Stopovers, 2039 Ninth Avenue, Ronkonkoma, NY 11779.

Asian Bucket Shops

Because few charters and no cut-rate upstarts ply the lengthy transpacific routes, off-price dealers in unofficially discounted tickets to the Orient flourish in Asian neighborhoods on the West Coast and in New York. The surplus of seats on Asian national flag carriers serving these routes prompted the airlines to allot a portion of their inventory to neighborhood travel services.

Until recently, off-price ethnic agents were a somewhat inscrutable Oriental secret. In order to restrict their clientele to the ethnic community and thus force nonethnics to pay full fare to the airlines themselves or to ordinary travel agents, these bucket shops advertised only in foreign-language Asian publications and operated from shops that displayed price lists in Oriental script.

Ethnic travel agents now operate openly and run English-language advertisements for deeply discounted transpacific fares on a variety of Asian flag carriers. Substantial discounts are available from Korean Air, China Airlines (Taiwan), Philippine Airlines; less dramatic ones are available from Singapore Airlines, Japan Airlines, and on some U.S. carriers flying Pacific routes.

For example, in the summer of 1986, the published round-trip excursion fare from New York to Hong Kong was $1,099, but discounters were selling it for around $700 (fares fluctuate seasonally and vary among dealers); the New York–Singapore fare is officially $1,349 and around $800 from discounters. The official Los Angeles/San Francisco–Tokyo APEX fare was $927, but you could buy it from a bucket shop for around $600. Good fares are also available for flights from New York or the West Coast to Bangkok, Manila, Taipei, Sydney, and Auckland.

Once you know what to look for, ethnic bucket shops are easy to spot. Many are advertised in the daily classified section of the San Francisco *Chronicle* under "Tours-Travel" and in the Sunday travel sections of the *Los Angeles Times, Chicago Tribune,* and the *New York Times.* The *Village Voice* regularly runs display ads for several New York-based agencies.

In San Francisco you can let your feet do the walking. Several firms are located in the Downtown Center Building at 165 O'Farrell Street, which looks like the place where Sam Spade kept his office. Chinatown is another fertile area, with a dozen or more firms occupying first- or second-floor offices within a block of the intersection of Clay Street and Waverly Place (a half block west of Grant Avenue). You can try contacting these agents by phone (Tokyo Travel, 415-989-3701; Shogun Travel, 415-397-1100; Jeanette's Travel Service, 415-397-2343; Canaan Travel Service, 415-421-4071). Keep in mind that the language may prove to be a barrier only a personal appearance can surmount.

Ethnic bucket shops operating out of New York include Apex Travel (800-428-8848; 212-661-1606), Sudo Tours (212-302-2860), Maharaja Travel (800-223-6862; 212-391-0122), and Globe Travel (718-539-3385). In Chicago try McSon Travel (800-622-1421; 312-346-6272).

Regular travel agents in any locale can handle off-price fares to Asia by working through wholesale suppliers. They may charge slightly more than ethnic agents, but the convenience of dealing with someone trustworthy who is also nearby is worth the added cost. Ask your travel agent whether he or she can write this kind of ticket.

TRADE-OFFS:	
Off-Price Travel Dealers	
Price: 60 percent off unrestricted economy, 30 percent off APEX fares	Principally available from major coastal gateways
	Availability fluctuates
Few advance-purchase, minimum/maximum-stay requirements	Limited selection of flight times
Full-frill scheduled airline service	Little flexibility to alter plans
	Tickets not transferable to other airlines
Can be used for last-minute travel, one-way routings	Possible problems with refunds and schedule changes
	May have to deal with small company in distant city

THE BRITISH CONNECTION

By making the British Connection, you get a London vacation and the opportunity to obtain airfare discounts of up to 70 percent off published fares to the rest of Europe and almost anywhere else in the world.

The effectiveness of the British Connection results from three factors: (1) low airfares and substantial service between the United States and London; (2) the relative strength of the U.S. dollar in comparison to the British pound; and (3) the proliferation and ompetitiveness of London bucket shops.

The London Shuttle

Low fares between the United States and London have been an institution since Freddie Laker rolled out the Skytrain. Laker may be gone, but his cut-price spirit lives on. Continental offers low-fare service from most U.S. cities via Newark and Denver. Virgin Atlantic charges from $219–$285 (depending on the season) for Same Day Saver tickets from Newark and Miami to London and from $349–$379 for normal economy.

The major airlines flying the route—TWA, Pan Am, British Airways, British Caledonian—offer day-of-departure standby fares intermittently throughout the year (see index for "Standby fares") usually for the same rate budget carriers charge—around $249 one way from New York; $349 from California. The major carriers' round-trip APEX fares—which bear substantial advance-purchase requirements and length-of-stay limitations—are usually less than $500. In addition, numerous charter flights and off-price scheduled fares are advertised in the travel sections of U.S. newspapers, particularly the Sunday *New York Times* and the *Village Voice*.

The Mighty Dollar

The value of the British Connection is ultimately contingent upon the exchange rate between the dollar and the pound. When the pound approaches parity with the dollar (as it did in early 1985), Americans can hardly afford to stay home. If the pound ever hits $2 again, you can shove this chapter right into the paper shredder. As long as it remains somewhere in the neighborhood of $1.65, the English Connection works. (Note: All London prices are expressed in pounds; consult the Foreign Exchange listings in a daily newspaper for the current exchange rate.)

London Bucket Shops

Much of the stock London bucket shops sell consists of tickets on national flag carriers on routes to places other than their home country, for example, Gulf Airways (United Arab Emirates) from London to Paris; Philippine Airlines to Rome; Alia (Jordan) to Singapore. Bucket shops also handle the surplus stock of such charter companies as Balair, a Swissair and British Airtours subsidiary. They also ticket obscure airlines that offer cheap fares to Europe.

In London bucket shops are legal, extremely conspicuous, and physically as well appointed as regular travel agencies. Street-level operations display their fares in the windows. Others advertise in the London dailies and in the weekly entertainment magazines, *Time Out* (60 pence at newsstands) and *London Alternative Magazine* (free in London shops).

In addition, some of the major full-service travel agencies have established separate discount units. Pickfords Travel operates Travelmart (238 City Road, London EC1; 01-253-1000), and Hogg Robinson Travel claims it can match or beat the fares at any bucket shop. Call the Air Travel Advisory Bureau (01-636-5000) for a referral to an agency that handles what you're after.

Bucket-Shop Fares

Here are some samples of the kind of deals London bucket shops offer. STA Travel (74 Brompton Road, London SW7; Intercontinental, 01-581-1022; Europe, 01-581-8233) has round trips to Munich for £74; Sydney, £629; Tel Aviv, £142; Singapore, £415; and Beijing, £456. Discount Travel Centre (216 Earls Court Road,

London SW5; 01-370-1146) advertises round-trip fares to Bangkok for £340; Delhi or Bombay, £360. Mundus Air Travel Limited (5 Peter Street, London W1V 3RR; 01-437-2272) specializes in cheap flights to Italy and Orion Travel (320 Upper Regent Street, London W1R 5AG; 01-580-3751) focuses on Greece, the Balearics, and Turkey.

Using a combination of air carriers to arrange low-priced round-the-world trips is another bucket-shop specialty. For £873, STA can book a London–Delhi or Bombay–Singapore–Sydney–Rarotonga–Nandi (Fiji Islands)–Tahiti–Honolulu–Los Angeles–London trip good for a full year. The Far East Travel Centre (3 Lower John Street, London W1A 4XE; 01-734-9318), which markets "tailor-made" trips through regular travel agencies, has a London–Hong Kong–Tokyo–Honolulu–Los Angeles–London round trip good for a year at a cost that ranges from £775 to £880 depending on the season. These are "off-the-peg" routings that can be modified for specific needs for somewhat higher fares.

Of course, Americans can terminate their excursions at a convenient U.S. destination and simply go home. Within one year of the first flight, the last coupon of the round-the-world ticket can be used to begin next year's British Connection.

Making the British Connection

London bucket shops are generally unwilling to write tickets below the published rate for flights from the United States to London or for flights that originate elsewhere than Great Britain; this is an illegal practice known as "cross-border ticketing." They are, however, willing to make bookings by phone and accept payment via charge cards.

For example, you can book trips out of London on STA Travel (01-581-1022) by phone with Visa or MasterCard and pick up your ticket when you arrive in London. The Travel Machine (7 Maddox Street, London, W1; 01-499-8366), which specializes in travel to Australia, New Zealand, and the Far East, will book over the phone and mail the tickets to the States.

Phone rates to London have decreased recently, and calling there (and elsewhere in Europe) probably costs less than you might expect. Between 7:00 A.M. and 1:00 P.M., the AT&T rate from New York to London is $1.65 for the first minute and $.99 for each additional minute; $1.23/$.75 between 1:00 P.M. and 6:00 P.M.; and $.99/$.60 between 6:00 P.M. and 7:00 A.M.

Since London is five hours ahead of the East Coast, their 9:00 to 5:00 business day corresponds to 4:00 A.M. to 12:00 noon in the Eastern time zone. Easterners can call London travel services between 4:00 A.M. and 7:00 A.M. at the lowest possible rates, paying only around $7.50 for a ten-minute call. Pacific time zone residents have an even longer range: They can call London at the cheapest rates between 1:00 A.M. and 7:00 A.M.

Other Bucket-Shop Locales

London is hardly the only city that boasts a thriving discount travel market. Equally good deals are available in Amsterdam, Brussels, Antwerp, and Athens, among many others. London is stressed, first, because it is the easiest European city for Americans to reach; and, secondly, because all transactions can be negotiated in English.

 TRADE-OFFS:
The London Connection

Low fares and numerous flights between the United States and London	Ticket availability limited during peak periods
The multitude of off-price tickets available from London to Europe and the rest of the world.	Danger of unscrupulous unregulated dealers
	Lack of flexibility
Limited or nonexistent advance-purchase, length-of-stay requirements	Value of British Connection fluctuates with the dollar
Last-minute travel possible	
Arrangements can be made by phone from the United States.	

 TRAVELER'S ALERT

Here are guidelines for buying off-price unofficially discounted tickets in the United States or abroad:

● Bucket shops usually deal in long-haul point-to-point international flights. Short-haul domestic and regional bargains are seldom available.

● Off-price fares are usually available only on little-known airlines with indirect routings and inconvenient schedules. You will seldom receive substantial discounts to routes where there is monopoly service—New York–Riyadh, for example, or anywhere behind the Iron Curtain.

● Don't expect to find bucket-shop fares during busy times or holiday weekends, when airlines can sell seats for normal fares.

- Airlines do not officially admit that off-price fares exist, so it is useless to ask for information about them. However, more and more regular travel agents are becoming familiar with and are willing to handle this kind of ticketing.

- Since bucket shops essentially set their own prices, there are substantial disparities in what different dealers charge for the same ticket. It's worth the trouble to shop around.

- Some off-price dealers cannot be trusted. *Time Out*, the London entertainment guide that prints reams of bucket-shop advertising, warns those in search of cheap flights to obtain written details of flights requested and any alternatives when paying a deposit; check whether, in the event of a cancellation, a full refund is forthcoming; and watch out for any extra charges and surcharges—all commissions should be included in the selling price.

  Time Out points out that "if you have any doubts about the flight you are being offered, do not part with any money until you have been informed of the name of the airline operating the flight (both outward and return), the airports of departure and destination and the date and time of flights. If the agent will not give this information, try another agent."

LAST-MINUTE TRAVEL CLUBS

A new breed of travel marketer known variously as "last-minute," "short-notice," "standby," or "flexible-schedule" clubs does for the travel industry what outlet stores do for the fashion industry. They take first-quality unsold merchandise from the "manufacturers"—in this case tour operators and cruise lines—and unload them at deep discounts.

Dealing mostly in cruises and complete package tours (including airfare, hotels and possibly some meals, sightseeing, and transfers), last-minute services are ideal for people with flexible schedules who want to get away but haven't decided where to go.

Joining the Club

Most last-minute marketers operate regionally as clubs with dues of $35 to $50 a year per household. Members receive club bulletins listing available trips and access to hotlines with recorded messages describing current offerings. If members hear something they like, they must call another number to book reservations for the trip.

The labels "last-minute," "standby," and "short-notice," however, are somewhat misleading. Although members cannot book very far in advance, most of the packaged tours depart within two to eight weeks. Cruises depart somewhat earlier—between one and four weeks. However, these outfits do occasionally offer air-only service on truly short notice, sometimes within a week.

Best Deals

The best last-minute deals involve tours to Europe in the summer, and year-round to the Caribbean and Hawaii. Prices vary with the destination and the quality of the package or cruise. And although members pay "close-out" prices, they get exactly the same quality of merchandise as those who pay "list."

Here are samples of the kinds of deals last-minute clubs offer: (Most prices are per person double; prices for singles are somewhat higher.)

● Ireland tour—fourteen days, airfare from New York and hotel. List price, $689; members, $199 (Vacations to Go)
● Disney World—seven days, airfare from Philadelphia plus hotel. List price $489; members, $169 (Discount Travel International)
● Caribbean cruise—seven days, from Fort Lauderdale. List price, $1,265; members, $699 (Worldwide Discount Travel Club)
● Acapulco package—seven days, airfare from Boston and hotels. List price, $632; members, $389 (Moment's Notice)
● Cancun—seven days, airfare from Cincinnati/Dayton/Columbus and hotel. List price, $509; members, $189 (Stand-Buys Ltd.)
● Detroit to Frankfurt—one or two weeks, airfare only. List price, $625; members $339 (Stand-Buys Ltd.)

Although the preponderance of European tours leave from New York and other northeast gateways, some last-minute clubs will arrange low-cost connecting flights to those locations. Also, it is not uncommon for cruises to include free airfare from various locales to the departure city.

Last-Minute Travel Clubs

Discount Travel International (Ives Building, Suite 205, Narbeth, PA 19072; 800-251-4900; 215-668-2182); $45/year per family. This club specializes in New York and northeast departures for European tours and cruises out of Florida; adding trips from the Midwest and the West Coast; members receive discounts on hotels, restaurants, car rentals, and attractions.

Last Minute Travel Company (132 Brookline Ave., Boston, MA 02215; 800-527-8646; 617-267-9800); $30/year per person; $35/year per couple. Last Minute Travel specializes in Boston and New York departures for Caribbean cruises and European tours.

Moment's Notice (40 East 49th Street, New York, NY 10017, 212-486-0503; and 1750 112th St. NE, Suite B112, Bellevue, WA 98004; 800-235-5800; 206-453-1180); $35/year per family. Moment's Notice concentrates on East Coast and some West Coast departures on European tours, Caribbean and Alaska cruises, and trips to Mexico.

On Call to Travel (14335 S.W. Allen Blvd., Suite 209, Beaverton, OR 97005; 503-643-7212); $39/year per household. This group provides West Coast—Seattle, Portland, San Francisco, Los Angeles—departures on tours and cruises to Hawaii, Europe, and Asia.

Sears Discount Travel Club (Dept. 404, 311 W. Superior Street, Chicago, IL 60610; 800-331-0257; in IL, 800-654-9492); $45/year per household. Array of programs includes "brief-notice" tours, cruises, and charter flights; "second-night-free" plan for 2,000 hotels in the U.S. and 25 foreign countries; discounts on long-range tours and cruises; "Condo-Saver" booking service for resort condos; car-rental discounts; custom trip planning and highway routing; and 5 percent rebates (in Sears gift certificates) for any standard travel purchased through the club.

South Florida Cruises (2069 North University Drive, Fort Lauderdale, FL 33323; 800-327-SHIP; 305-493-6300). No membership fee is required. Cruises are available at only up to 30 percent off from ports in Florida, the Northeast, and the West Coast.

Spur of the Moment Cruises (10780 Jefferson Boulevard, Culver City, CA 90230; 800-343-1991; in California, 800-233-2129; 213-839-2418). No membership fee is required. Cruises depart only from the West Coast and Florida.

Stand-Buys Limited (311 West Superior Street, #404, Chicago, IL 60610; 800-255-0200; in Illinois, 800-826-4398; 312-951-7589); $45/year per family. One of the oldest and largest of the last-minute clubs, Stand-Buys offers a diverse and unusual selection of cruises, tours, and air-only arrangements from various departure points.

Vacations to Go (2411 Fountain View, Houston, TX 77057; 800-624-7338; in Texas, 800-833-8047; 713-974-2121); $30/year per household (family plus one guest). This organization is headquartered in Houston but has branches in more than forty U.S. cities. It features a selection of packages and cruises from diverse starting points; low-fare arrangements to gateway cities are available.

Worldwide Discount Travel Club (1674 Meridian Avenue, Miami Beach, FL 33139; 305-534-2082); $35/year per individual; $50/year per family. Worldwide Discount specializes principally in cruises leaving from the East Coast and in European tours.

A new firm called **QuickTrips International** is forming a network of local travel agencies—one in every major city—to market close-out travel. Check local advertising for the name of the QuickTrips dealer in your area.

The great advantage of last-minute travel clubs is that they offer first-quality travel merchandise at discounts of as much as one-third of the retail price. But you can't wait until literally the last minute. You must start planning at least two or three weeks in advance. The small membership fee easily pays for itself the first time you use the service, and some clubs don't require you to join until you're ready to travel.

To accommodate this kind of vacation, you must sacrifice a degree of independence. You can neither plan your vacation very far in advance nor take off at the last minute. And you may not be able to find a convenient trip to a place you really want to visit.

Although these last-minute clubs occasionally offer air-only arrangements, their principal products are cruises and package tours—not everybody's cup of tea. (On some package tours, however, it may be profitable to buy the package for the airfare alone and in effect throw away the rest of the package.)

At this time, the preponderance of last-minute products is available out of New York and, to a lesser extent, California. Travelers in the rest of the country must make their way to a coastal gateway and, because of the last-minute nature of the arrangement, may not have time to qualify for the lowest airfares.

Some clubs extend the close-out sale metaphor to the point of offering merchandise completely "as is"—no refunds, alterations, or exchanges permitted.

TRADE-OFFS:
⊕ Last-Minute Discount Clubs ⊖

Low prices, up to 70 percent off the list price of tours and cruises	Product predominantly full package tours and cruises, not normally suitable for independent traveler
First-quality travel merchandise	
Not really—"last-minute"—bookable two to eight weeks in advance	Preponderance of products available from the coasts
	No flexibility in travel plans
Low membership fees, easily made up by first trip taken	Possible difficulty obtaining refunds or alterations
	Seldom usable for travel at the very last minute

FLYING AS A FREE-LANCE COURIER

Back in discount airfare prehistory—long before Ultra-Savers, Moonlight Specials, or People Express—the very existence of courier flights was a closely held secret. Information was strictly a word-of-mouth proposition; key phone numbers were passed among trusted friends sworn to silence lest the word seep out and spoil it for the cognoscenti.

The big secret was that people could fly on airplanes absolutely free. They could fly free to faraway places—from coast to coast, to Florida, even to Europe. It was completely legal, and all they had to do was practically nothing.

The Golden Age

I became aware of courier flights one day in 1977 when my brother turned up at the door claiming he had just flown in from San Francisco for free. He spoke of mysterious organizations called air courier companies, whose business was sending things—nice things like documents, small packages, and videotapes, not, as some have aspersed, narcotics or tainted currency—across the country overnight on scheduled airlines. A fortuitous confluence of circumstance made it advantageous for courier companies to send these shipments as baggage accompanying their own people or, barring that, any outsider who would make the trip.

To set up a trip you had to call the number provided by your source and ask for "Sally" or "Chico" or whoever happened to be in charge of the program. Using your source as a makeshift character reference, you would tell Sally or Chico that you wanted to fly, say, from Los Angeles to Chicago on Friday and ask if a courier was needed. If the answer was yes, you discussed terms, arranged to meet, and would indeed fly from Los Angeles to Chicago for free.

Modern Times

Unfortunately, somebody squealed. Word got around. Information about courier flights began appearing in the press and in books (ah-hem) on low-cost travel, and the rest is history.

The good news is that the existence and credibility of courier services is now so well documented that finding them and arranging travel is much easier. The bad news is that barring a few rare exceptions, courier flights aren't free anymore. Courier firms now expect free-lance couriers to pay at least part of the cost of the plane ticket.

LAST-MINUTE TRAVEL CLUBS

NAME AND ADDRESS	PHONE	MEMBERSHIP FEE	SPECIALTY
Discount Travel International Ives Building, Suite 205 Narbeth, PA 19072	800-251-4900 215-668-2182	$45/year per family	NY and Northeast departures to Europe; cruises from Florida; adding trips from Midwest, West Coast; member discounts on hotels, car-rentals, restaurants, etc.
Last Minute Travel Company 132 Brookline Ave. Boston, MA 02215	617-267-9800 800-527-8646	$35/year per couple	Boston, New York departures for Caribbean cruises, European tours
Moment's Notice 40 E. 49th Street New York, NY 10017	212-486-0503 206-625-0900 800-235-5800	$35/year per family	Mostly East Coast, some West Coast departures on European tours, Caribbean, Alaska cruises
On Call to Travel 14335 S.W. Allen Blvd. Suite 209 Beaverton, OR 97005	503-643-7212	$39/year per household	West Coast departures for tours and cruises to Hawaii, Europe, Asia
Sears Discount Travel Club 311 W. Superior Street, Dept. 404 Chicago, IL 60610	800-331-0257 in IL, 800-654-9492	$45/year per family	"Brief-notice" tours, cruises, and charters; second-night-free hotel program; rebates on regularly-priced travel; and numerous other benefits

Company	Phone	Fee	Description
South Florida Cruises 2069 N. University Drive Fort Lauderdale, FL 33323	800-327-SHIP 305-493-6300	None	Cruises from Florida, Northeast, West Coast
Spur of the Moment Cruises 10780 Jefferson Boulevard Culver City, CA 90203	800-343-1991 In CA, 800-233-2129 213-839-2418	None	Cruises only from West Coast and Florida
Stand-Buys Limited 311 W. Superior Street, #404 Chicago, IL 60610	800-826-4398 In IL, 800-255-0200 312-951-7589	$45/year per family	Cruises, tours, air-only deals from various departure points
Vacations to Go 2411 Fountain View Houston, TX 77057	800-624-7338 In TX, 800-833-8047 713-974-2121	$30/year per household	Headquartered in Houston, branches in more than 40 U.S. cities; packages and cruises from diverse departure points; low-fare arrangements to gateways
Worldwide Discount Travel Club 1674 Meridian Avenue Miami Beach, FL 33139	305-534-2082	$50/year per family	Cruises from East Coast, European tours

The Cheapest Way to Fly

Although the cost of courier flights is somewhat contingent upon normal coach fares and seasonal demand for couriers, courier flights normally cost drastically less than normal coach and somewhat less than the lowest advance-purchase discount fare. Some recent examples: New York to Los Angeles, $75 one way; New York to London, $140 one way; Chicago to London, $200 one way; New York to Paris, $450 round trip. (Couriers usually have the option of flying one way or round trip.) Despite public knowledge and a rash of greed among courier firms, a courier flight is still the cheapest way to travel.

The Air-Courier Business

The business of an air-courier company is overnight delivery of time-sensitive documents, tapes, and other items. Large companies like Federal Express and United Parcel operate their own fleets of planes. Smaller firms rely on regularly scheduled air carriers. They buy coach tickets and use a passenger's free baggage allowance for their cargo. In addition, the courier firm pays for excess baggage at a favorable rate. Also important for the courier firm, is the fact that because the cargo is officially traveling as checked baggage, it (and you) will not be "bumped" from the flight.

Because the courier firm uses the entire free-baggage allowance plus substantial additional paid-for baggage used by the courier firm, *free-lance couriers are limited to carry-on baggage.* Although recent security considerations may change this situation, domestic airlines have been fairly liberal about what they allow passengers to carry onboard planes. International flights are more strict about enforcing carry-on baggage rules. Before you fly as an international courier, check out the airline's carry-on policies and comply with them.

Courier Duties

Apart from baggage limitations and the occasional requirement to hand-carry extra-sensitive material, a courier's responsibilities are next to nil. Having paid the courier firm in advance for the ticket, the courier will meet a representative of the company either at the company's office or at the airport. The courier then receives his or her ticket and claim checks for baggage that in most instances the representative has already checked.

On arrival at the appointed destination, the courier has to locate a representative of the firm, turn over the claim checks, and go his merry way. More often than not, couriers never lay eyes on the cargo—usually canvas sacks filled with parcels—for which they have been responsible.

On international flights the procedure is somewhat more complicated. One reason for using free-lance couriers on international flights is that customs processes checked baggage more quickly than unaccompanied freight. Consequently, the courier must stay at the airport until the baggage has actually cleared customs. This procedure normally takes from forty-five to sixty minutes, but I know from experience that it can take considerably longer.

The courier is officially responsible for the contents of the cargo and the propriety of the paperwork accompanying it. Courier firms have always insisted that there is no possibility of a courier being detained (or arrested!) for transporting contraband, and I have never found any reason to doubt them.

Limitations

One limitation of free-lance courier flying is that *only a handful of major destinations are involved.* Domestically, these are New York, Chicago, Denver, Los Angeles, San Francisco, Miami, and Houston. Internationally, major destinations are London, Madrid, Zurich, Milan, and Hong Kong. Although couriers occasionally go to just about anywhere, these are the centers of major action.

Another disadvantage is that courier companies almost inevitably take the last flight of the day to their destination. Arriving late, the courier has a limited (and possibly expensive) range of airport transportation and lodging options. Also, by taking the last flight out there's no alternative way to reach your destination that day if, as occasionally happens, the deal doesn't go down.

Locating Courier Flights

One way to track down a courier company is to let your fingers do the walking. Most classified phone directories list them under "Air Courier Service" (the Manhattan Consumer Yellow Pages lists sixty firms). Some of the larger nationwide courier firms are TNT Skypak, DHL, Securicor, Archer, and On Board.

Call the courier services listed for your departure city and ask if they need a free-lance courier to your desired destination. Some firms use only their own people or trusted referrals; others happily enlist any warm body willing to make the flight. Courier firms constantly fall in and out of love with free-lancers, however, and the firm that used free-lancers last year may have sworn off them by the next time you call. Start looking for courier flights as far in advance as possible. And be prepared to take many no's for answers.

Some courier firms advertise for couriers in daily newspapers and in "alternative" publications such as the *Village Voice* in New York and the *Reader* in Chicago and Los Angeles. The *New York Times* lists ads for couriers under "Public and Commercial Notices"; other papers include them in the classified section under "Travel," "Transportation," or "Tickets."

PTC Tours (225 West 34th Street, New York, NY 10122; 212-760-0310) regularly advertises courier flights from New York to London and Paris. And some of the one- or two-column–inch display ads placed by off-price travel dealers in the travel section of the Sunday *New York Times* and in the *Village Voice* (See Index for "Off-price Travel Dealers") may lead to a courier flight. In responding to those ads, I've been offered the option of flying as a courier or paying $25 more to take the same flight as a regular passenger.

In any event, the deal is sealed the moment the would-be courier pays for the flight. An easily negotiable form of payment —cash, money order, traveler's check, certified check—is usually required.

Courier Agents

Another way to book a courier flight is through aeronautical matchmakers known as courier agents. Courier agents make arrangements for a large number of firms that need many free-lance couriers to a variety of places on a regular basis.

The advantage of working with an agent is that they offer many more flights than any single courier firm. They do the legwork and also handle all of the paperwork. Courier agents, unlike the firms, may accept charge cards. Courier agents also provide a modicum of personalized attention: Tell them you want to fly to Milan some time in April and if something comes up they're likely to call you. Try that with a courier firm and they're likely to laugh in your face.

The one disadvantage is that you must pay a registration fee to partake of their services.

Sandman Express was a heavily promoted Los Angeles-based firm that temporarily coordinated an extensive network of domestic and international courier flights. Since it went out of business in early 1985, the only established courier agent is a New York operation named after an old Bette Davis flick, Now Voyager.

Now Voyager screens couriers and regularly books flights between New York and Los Angeles ($150 round trip), Miami ($60 round trip), Madrid ($200 round trip), Milan ($300 round trip), Amsterdam ($199 round trip), London ($250 round trip), Hong Kong ($300 round trip), Paris ($300 round trip), Rio de Janeiro ($300 round trip), and Sydney ($600 round trip). Flights are also frequently available to Mexico City, Buenos Aires, Frankfurt, and Bermuda. Prices are subject to seasonal fluctuation but seldom exceed half of the lowest available discount fare.

Now Voyager is always trying to add new names to its Footloose List, people whose life-styles allow them to leave on short notice or no notice to irregular Now Voyager destinations—among them Geneva, Honolulu, Brussels, and Ankara. These flights cost even less than normal Now Voyager deals. The Footloose List includes students, retirees, teachers on summer vacation or sabbatical, or others ready to fly at a moment's notice. If you're reasonably footloose, mention it when you call or write it on your application. Now Voyager also operates special programs in which couriers fly for free and, in some cases, get paid.

Now Voyager currently charges a $45 a year registration fee; contact the firm at 74 Varick Street, Suite 307, New York, NY 10013; 212-431-1616, Monday through Friday, noon to 5:00 P.M. Eastern time.

Courier-Flight Pitfalls

Having explained the why's and how's of free-lance courier flying, it's my duty to report that this is not a particularly reliable form of low-cost travel. One year I arranged for four courier flights. Two came off without a hitch. Two never happened.

In one case, the courier firm failed to make the airport rendezvous. When I called from the airport to inquire, I was told that the flight had been changed and another courier engaged. If I still wanted to fly that day, a rude and totally unconcerned clerk suggested that I walk up to the counter and buy a ticket.

The other mishap occurred when a change in the company's booking procedures resulted in two couriers, myself and a young lady, showing up at the office for the same flight. The firm washed its hands of the matter and left it to us to sort out whose claim was paramount. (The young lady offered me a modest emolument and flew.)

Fear of Not Flying

I do not contend that my experience was typical or that my 50 percent success ratio reflects any sort of industry average. But there are always risks of not flying, and they stem from the nature of the courier business.

The unreliability of courier flights results in part from the unpredictability of the overnight air-freight business. Occasionally there isn't enough cargo to justify sending a courier. It also results from the company's attitude toward free-lancers. Some firms are businesslike, polite, and helpful; others think free-lance couriers fall somewhere between panhandlers and child molesters, and treat them accordingly. Consequently, it would not occur to them to inform a courier when a flight has been canceled or changed.

One particularly mistrustful firm arranges to have couriers board with only a boarding pass—no ticket coupon. This prevents the wily courier from cashing in the ticket and heading for the hills. Flying as a free-lance courier is located in the nether reaches of the dignity scale where, for many of us, potential savings cease to be "worth it."

Pros and Cons

The pro side of flying as a free-lance courier is cost—it's simply the cheapest way to fly. Even today you could still get lucky and fly for free.

Because the cargo must go through, you fly on the most reliable airlines and receive full in-flight services. It is also possible to take advantage of courier-size savings by flying at the last minute. In some cases, couriers can apply courier flight mileage to airline frequent-flyer programs, and it is not utterly unknown for couriers to hitch rides on supersonic Concordes.

On the con side, few seats are available and these are particularly hard to get during peak flying seasons and on weekends. Routings are very limited. Fares are sometimes barely less than those of regular carriers. Couriers have no flexibility to alter flights and no one to complain to if things go wrong. Couriers usually fly late-night flights. Then there is the "dignity factor" and, despite everything, the real possibility that you might not fly at all.

As a *Cheap/Smart Travel* alternative, flying as a free-lance courier has limited viability. I have flown as a courier, and I would do so again. But I would not consider it in situations when, to paraphrase the courier's courier, Federal Express, I absolutely positively have to be there. And whenever I used it I would arrange another form of low-cost transportation as a contingency plan to cover my proverbial posterior.

TRADE-OFFS:
⊕ Free-Lance Courier Flights ⊖

⊕	⊖
Price—from free to well below the lowest discount fare	Few seats available
Reliable full-frill scheduled airlines	Limited selection of routings
One-way or round-trip flights available	No choice of flight times
Advance booking and last-minute arrangements possible	No flexibility to alter plans
	Possibility that you may not fly
	No recourse for mishaps
	No baggage check
	Late-night flights
	Dignity factor

GETTING BUMPED INTO FREE FLIGHTS

It is with some selfish hesitation that I share this information on *the only way to fly for free*. Why? Because the opportunities for doing so are limited and the greater the number of people who get in on it, the less likely it becomes that any of them will take advantage of the situation. So be it . . .

Denied-Boarding Compensation

Bumping—denied boarding—occurs when there are more passengers with confirmed reservations who show up for a flight than there are seats on the plane. This is called overbooking the plane. Airlines overbook because they know from experience that all passengers who have made reservations seldom show up for the flight. To have any chance of filling the plane, airline computers estimate the number of passengers likely to be no-shows and accept reservations accordingly.

Airlines usually guess right—fewer than 20 of every 10,000 passengers are voluntarily or involuntarily bumped. But when they make a mistake, they are obliged to pay the price. (They are not, however, obliged to offer compensation when flights are canceled because of weather conditions, changes in aircraft, such as when a smaller plane is substituted for a larger one, on planes with sixty or fewer passengers, or on flights originating outside the United States.)

For a businessperson rushing to close a deal, getting bumped is unalloyed disaster. For those with the flexibility to take advantage of such travel boondoggles as come their way, getting bumped—and compensated—is an unalloyed windfall.

Call for Volunteers

Realizing that some passengers are better disposed than others to handle denied boarding, an airline that has oversold a flight will request volunteers to renounce their seats. Since the airline doesn't expect passengers to volunteer out of the kindness of their hearts, it usually offers a guaranteed seat on the next available flight plus additional compensation.

Compensation usually consists of free travel. Some carriers offer vouchers good for free confirmed round-trip coach travel to any domestic destination in the airline's route system. Usually this type of voucher must be redeemed within one year. Sometimes airlines offer vouchers in dollar amounts which can be applied toward the cost of purchasing a ticket or tickets in any class and at any fare level within the carrier's domestic and international system. Initially, the airline may offer vouchers worth $300; if no one steps forward, they keep raising the ante until volunteers materialize. Vouchers have been distributed for as much as $2,000 worth of travel. Eventually, however, it's no more Mr. Nice. The airline starts bumping passengers involuntarily, choosing either late check-ins or discount fare holders and forcing on them the compensation offered to volunteers.

Case Histories

My first bump occurred on a Sunday afternoon Piedmont flight from Charlotte to Newark. Just prior to boarding, an airline representative announced that the flight was oversold and that volunteers who relinquished their seats would receive a guaranteed seat on a flight to Newark two hours later plus a voucher good for round-trip travel to any Piedmont destination. The voucher would be valid for "positive space" (reserved, not standby) and could be used anytime within a year.

It sounded good to me, so I rushed forward to beat the stampede—which, surprisingly, never came. Only four passengers volunteered, and Piedmont ultimately had to bump a nonvolunteer. I received a travel voucher and boarding pass for the next flight (which I would have gladly volunteered to miss if the occasion had arisen) and considered it the luckiest day of my life. For reading magazines for two hours of a Sunday afternoon in the Charlotte Airport, I would get an absolutely free trip to California, Denver, Texas, or anywhere else Piedmont flew.

What I strongly suspect is that an error on the part of ground personnel made me "victim" to another felicitous bump. Because

I had a business appointment at the airport, I checked in two hours early for an afternoon People Express flight from Syracuse to Newark. Without checking to see whether I had a reservation, the "Customer Service Manager"—that catchall People Express title —gave me a boarding pass. It was number four under the People Express system of numbering boarding passes in order of check-in. Returning at flight time, I glimpsed the familiar People Express swarm at the podium and began to think bumping.

As number four, I boarded early and watched eagerly as the plane filled. When every seat was occupied, a CSM began, "Well, it seems that we made sort of a mistake and have a few more passengers than seats so. . . ." At which point I switched on the overhead call light and began gathering my things.

As with Piedmont, the compensation was a voucher for round-trip travel to any domestic People Express destination (People Express vouchers became valid on Continental after the merger). My prognosis is that the check-in clerks had erred by giving boarding passes to people without reservations when the flight looked as if it would be empty. When reservation holders eventually showed up, they had no choice but to solicit volunteers.

How to Get Bumped

Statistically, the chances of getting bumped are approximately 600 to 1. Those are long odds, but insofar as this means that for every two 747s or four 727s that take off full at least one passenger gets a freebie, it's worth taking a shot.

• *Choose your flight.* Flights are most heavily booked on Friday and Sunday evenings, making these the best probable-bumping times. Holiday weekends, in other respects the absolute worst time to fly, are bonanzas for would-be bumpees. Almost every flight is overbooked during major holidays, when it is common to see signs posted in airports offering compensation to those willing to take later flights.

• *Choose your airline.* Since each carrier determines its own margin on overbookings, the choice of airline makes a big difference. While waiting for the next Piedmont flight to Newark, another of the "volunteers" told me that he flew Piedmont regularly and they nearly always overbooked. Statistically, other high bumpers include Continental and Pan Am. The airlines with the lowest bumping rates are American, Eastern, United, Northwest, and US Air.

• *Avoid bumps in the night.* What you want least is to get bumped off the airline's last flight of the day. You have to stay overnight if this happens, and even if the airline does provide a hotel room (sometimes they do, sometimes they don't), it puts a major cramp in your plans. The best solution is to avoid booking on the airline's last flight of the day to your destination. Give yourself the leeway of at least a flight or two. And always have a timetable on hand so you are fully aware of all the options.

● *Rigorously comply with the airline's check-in requirements.* In most cases this means showing up at the boarding gate at least ten minutes prior to departure. If you are late, your reservation will be canceled and you may not fly at all, much less receive compensation.

● *Stay alert.* Hover around the podium before boarding, ready to spring into action at the first call for volunteers.

● *Volunteer to volunteer.* If it looks as if the flight might be overbooked, tell the check-in clerk you're willing to give up your seat. Airline personnel will thank you for this, because the only thing they find more distasteful than soliciting volunteers is bumping passengers involuntarily. The clerk may hold on to your boarding pass. If it turns out they're overbooked, you've already volunteered. If they aren't overbooked, the boarding pass is returned and you fly.

● *Do not despair even after you board.* A miscount may result in a request for volunteers from passengers who are already seated.

Using the Voucher

To use your travel voucher you can make a reservation by phone, but you usually have to bring the voucher to the airline itself—not a travel agent—for ticketing. To do this, you can go to an in-town ticket office or wait until you reach the airport.

One of the great aspects of denied-boarding compensation vouchers is that you can use them at any time during the year. That means you can fly for free when it's already too late to qualify for advance-purchase discounts. And you can fly free during holiday periods when discount seats are limited and booked well in advance. Some vouchers are not transferable: they must be used by the bumpees who may have to show identification to be ticketed. Other vouchers are transferable and may be given away, bartered, or sold to the highest bidder. In fact, some dealers at airports purchase transferable vouchers for cash on the spot, while others solicit vouchers in classified ads: Check out the "Travel," "Transportation," and "Tickets" sections of local dailies and the "Discount Travel" classifieds of *USA Today*.

$\oplus$	TRADE-OFFS: Getting Bumped	$\ominus$
Free flights to numerous destinations at a time of your choice Vouchers valid for last-minute and peak-period travel Delays of usually no more than two or three hours		Remote chance of getting bumped on most flights Chances improved only by flying at most chaotic times Potential of lengthy waits and schedule disruptions until next flight

FREQUENT-FLYER PROGRAMS

Frequent-flyer bonus programs were one of the first institutional changes wrought by the Airline Deregulation Act. It began in 1981, when American Airlines introduced the AAdvantage program awarding free flights to passengers who accumulated various levels of mileage on American.

The AAdvantage plan did more than encourage "brand loyalty" among frequent business travelers—then and now the airlines' best customer. It also learned their names, addresses, corporate titles, and kept minute track of their flight activity—information that would be crucial for determining the restrictions on discount ticketing that would thwart business-traveler use of them.

United quickly kept pace with Mileage Plus, and TWA introduced the Frequent-Flyer Bonus program. They were originally announced as experimental programs with cut-off dates for earning mileage credits. But apparently the experiment worked and frequent-flyer programs have become as popular—and probably as permanent—an airline institution as "coffee, tea, or milk."

Today almost all major and regional U.S. and Canadian airlines, plus a number of foreign carriers, operate some sort of bonus program (see p. 89). And even if you are not what the airlines or anyone else would characterize as a frequent flyer, there are excellent reasons for participating.

Earning Free Flights

Frequent-flyer programs are the green stamps of the sky: The more miles you pay for, the more you fly for free. And although airlines are constantly adjusting the mileage levels required for various awards, a few generalizations can be made.

● The lowest award (10,000 miles on most of the major airlines) is usually a first-class upgrade: the right to fly first class on your coach ticket.

● The next strata of awards, usually within the 20,000- to 35,000-mile range, include a selection of increasingly deep discounts off standard fares—from 25 percent to 75 percent. At this level, some airlines also offer free "companion tickets"—freebies for someone accompanying a paying customer.

● Above 40,000 miles, awards get serious: free round-trip transportation in first class or coach, both domestic and international—the sky being the limit. The ultimate award is available on the Pan Am WorldPass program: Passengers who accrue 225,000 miles receive two passes for thirty days of unlimited, worldwide first-class travel.

● Most airlines black out use of award certificate flights during peak travel periods, usually New Year's, Easter/Spring vacation, July 4, Labor Day, Thanksgiving, and Christmas.

Earthly Rewards

Free flights are but the tip of the frequent-flyer plan iceberg. The programs now represent complex and constantly shifting alliances between the airlines and car-rental firms, hotel chains, cruise companies, foreign air carriers, commuter carriers, and their own domestic competitors.

AAdvantage members, for example, can use mileage awards to fly on KLM, Singapore, Qantas, or British Airways; rent Avis cars; and obtain discounts or free stays at Inter-Continental, Wyndham, Forum, and Sheraton hotels. Continental/Eastern OnePass participants can use mileage to fly on Alitalia, Aer Lingus, Air France, British Caledonian, Sabena, or SAS; stay in Compri, Doubletree, Marriott, Radisson, Regent International, Southern Pacific, and Wyndham Hotels; and drive General, Hertz, Europcar, Thrifty, and Tilden rent-a-cars.

Along with tie-ins for spending bonus awards, participants can also earn frequent-flyer mileage by renting the right car and sleeping in the right hotel. Delta frequent flyers accumulate mileage (a minimum of 1,000 miles per flight) by taking commuter flights on Atlantic Southeast, Comair, Sky West, and Business Express, plus Air Canada, Lufthansa, Swissair, Japan Air Lines, and Air New Zealand. United Mileage Plus participants earn a 750-mile bonus each time they rent a car from Hertz or Budget, 1,000–1,250 miles for each day on a Holland American cruise ship, a 500-mile mileage bonus for stays in Westin, Hyatt, or Kempinski hotels.

These airline/hotel/car-rental/cruise-line alliances are in constant flux. The only way to keep up with them is through advertising and the periodic newsletters most airlines send to participants.

Racking up Mileage

Most airlines base awards on air mileage. At first the awards were made according to the actual miles flown, a practice that tended to encourage zealous participants to fly from Seattle to Los Angeles by way of Oshkosh if they could get away with it. Now most carriers ignore specific routings and award bonuses on the basis of point-to-point mileage between starting and finishing points.

In the coach (or economy) section, the fare paid for the ticket has no relevance to the mileage award. Participants flying on the deepest discount receive the same mileage credit as those who purchase full-fare tickets. Business-class and first-class passengers receive bonuses of between 110 percent and 200 percent of the coach mileage.

Most carriers offer minimum mileage awards for any flight, usually in the 500- to 1,000-mile range. In addition, airlines constantly run double or triple mileage specials to introduce new routes, combat competition from upstarts on traditional routes, and drum up traffic during slack seasons. These bonuses are announced in the newsletters, special mailings, and through advertising.

Not for Frequent Flyers Only

Chances are you are *not* the sort of passenger the airlines set their caps for when they devised frequent-flyer programs. Airlines define a frequent flyer as someone who takes at least twelve trips a year. Only about a million people travel that much, but an estimated seven million Americans belong to frequent-flyer programs.

If you aren't a frequent flyer, your chances of earning free flights are slim. For a domestic round-trip ticket, the major carriers require from 20,000 miles (Northwest, US Air) to 50,000 miles (American). Since a New York–Los Angeles flight is 2,469 miles, you would have to fly the equivalent of more than four transcontinental round trips to qualify for the 20,000-mile programs and over ten for the 50,000-mile plans.

But even if you are a relatively infrequent flyer or never fly at all, membership in frequent-flyer programs can do a lot for you. First, there are no qualifications for joining, no application is ever refused, and (except for the Pan Am, $25 a year and Air Canada, $20) membership in frequent-flyer programs is free. To enroll, pick up an application onboard a flight, at the airport or airline ticket office; or call the airline's toll-free reservations number to request one.

Soft Touches

While the major carriers don't start passing out the awards you really want—free flights—until you've logged 35,000 or 50,000 miles, some of the smaller lines are softer touches. The Northwest WorldPerks and US Air Frequent Traveler programs are "cheapest": A mere 20,000 miles earns a free domestic roundtrip. Midway treats Flyer's First members to a free round-trip ticket after ten round trips. At 5,000 miles, Alaska Airlines forks over an upgrade to first class plus a one-gram gold ingot. At the 10,000-mile level, you get an upgrade to first class on American, Piedmont, TWA, Continental, Eastern, Delta, and United, and $25 off the initiation fee to the US Air Club, private lounges in seven airports.

Other Participant Perks

Another incentive for joining frequent-flyer programs is that participants qualify for car-rental discounts when they fly a particular airline, another airline, or don't fly at all. Hertz offers discounts to participants of ten different frequent-flyer programs. Avis, Budget, National, Thrifty, and Alamo have also forged discount alliances with numerous air carriers.

Infrequent flyers can also qualify for other types of preaward privileges. The formula for determining the priority of passengers wait listed for flights takes into account a number of factors: the type of fare paid, whether you are an originating or connecting passenger (connecting is better), and the time you checked in for the flight. Some carriers also include membership in the airline frequent-flyer club as a factor in the formula.

TWA offers members flying any class a selection of special menus unavailable to other passengers. United and Delta offer their frequent flyers the right to purchase first-class upgrades at nominal rates on a space-available basis. United participants flying on some discount fares also get advance seat assignment, a privilege now denied non-member discount passengers.

As a goodwill gesture after a 1985 pilots strike, United granted Mileage Plus participants two months of free upgrades on full-fare coach fares. United also magnanimously credited its members with mileage flown on United routes over competing carriers during the strike.

AIRLINES WITH FREQUENT-FLYER BONUS PROGRAMS

Air Cal	Hawaiian
Air Canada	Japan Air Lines
Alaska Airlines	Korean Air
All Nippon Airways	Lufthansa
Aloha Airlines	Midway
American	Midwest Express
America West	Northwest Orient
Avianca	Pan Am
BWIA	Philippine Airlines
Canadian Airlines International (CP Air)	Piedmont
	Sabena
Cayman Airways	Southwest
Continental/Eastern	Thai International
Delta	TWA
El Al	United
Finnair	US Air
Empire	Virgin Atlantic

A Word of Caution

Beware lest the lure of the riches of bonus awards entice you to pay *too* much more for your airfare. Business travelers can learn the ropes of accumulating frequent-flyer mileage because the boss pays the tuition. For those of us who travel on our own money, paying slightly higher fares to win a future free trip can be a good investment. Paying a lot more, however, serves the purpose of airline marketing departments but sorely defeats ours.

TRADE-OFFS:
⊕ Frequent-Flyer Programs ⊖

Chance to earn free flights and other benefits	Temptation to pay higher fares to accumulate mileage
Car-rental discounts	
No membership fee	

MILEAGE AWARD-CERTIFICATE BROKERS

Believe it or not, for many of the frequent flyers who accumulate the megamileage required to win awards, a free airplane ride is not exactly Christmas in July. Many frequent flyers would prefer to be rewarded for conspicuous brand loyalty with coin of the realm. Since the airlines permit award winners to transfer free flights to other parties, there now exists a secondary market of brokers who buy award certificates from frequent flyers and sell them to passengers looking for bargains.

Mileage-Award Customers

Basically mileage-award brokers sell certificates to *first-class or business-class travelers who can save up to 50 percent on flights to Europe and the Far East.* A first-class round-trip ticket between the United States and Europe costs from $4,000 to $5,000; frequent-flyer awards applicable to flights on this route usually cost in the neighborhood of $1,500. Smaller savings are also available on domestic transcon flights.

Transfer Procedures

Although each airline has its own way of doing things, transfer procedures follow the same general pattern. A frequent-flyer award recipient sells the award to the broker but does not designate the name of the person to whom the award is transferred. When the broker finds a customer for the award the award recipient signs the certificate over to the buyer and sends it to the broker. The broker then has the buyer ticketed at a cooperating travel agency and sends the ticket to the customer. Since many airlines now forbid travel agents to ticket frequent-flyer certificates, customers may have to do the ticketing themselves.

On carriers that allow awards to be transferred immediately, the buyer can receive his or her ticket and travel right away. Other carriers—generally those distributing coveted first-class international certificates—insist that the certificates be returned to them for transfer, a procedure that can take up to four or five weeks. In other words, mileage-award certificate purchasers may be subject to advance-purchase requirements ranging from zip to five weeks.

Legal, But Not Kosher

Buying mileage-award certificates is not illegal, but it does violate the letter of some airlines' rules. Suspecting that the award certificate trade was starting to tap into the lucrative market of business travelers, the airlines have begun making concerted efforts to crack down on brokering. In late 1986, American, TWA, and United jointly sued the Coupon Bank of San Diego, charging illegal practices. And instead of permitting travel agents to ticket for award certificates, several airlines—among them Delta, Northwest, and TWA—now allow only their own offices to do ticketing. In most cases, these award certificates are non-transferable or transferable only to persons with the same last name as the award recipient.

By way of throwing a soaking wet blanket on the proceedings, Northwest has been placing this slice of heaven among ads for certificate brokers in newspapers and magazines: "WARNING!! Northwest and Republic Airlines Frequent Flyer Awards are void if sold. If you purchase or sell a Northwest or Republic Airlines free travel award it is subject to confiscation by Northwest and you will be liable for payment of a full fare." Such confiscations have on occasion taken place.

Another drawback to this practice is that tickets written from mileage-award certificates are *un*endorsable, which means that they can't be used on other carriers flying the same route. If your airline cancels a flight, you have to wait for the next one. You can change flight times on these tickets, but you can't obtain refunds. You can, however, try to sell the ticket to someone who is willing to fly under your name.

Mileage-award certificate brokers offer potential airfare savings but only in special circumstances. Middle-market travelers can use brokers effectively when they have no option to paying the full coach fare, a four-figure round-trip purchase on the longest domestic routes. Generally speaking, the standard discount programs are easier, more flexible, and less expensive.

Finding Mileage-Award Brokers

Mileage-award brokers advertise in *USA Today*, the *Wall Street Journal*, *New York Times*, Los Angeles *Times*, and *Washington Post*. Although several of the oldest established have gone out of business, many are still going strong. The American Coupon Exchange in Newport Beach, CA, and elsewhere (714-644-4112 in the west; 212-319-4600 in the east); Travel Discounts International, New York (212-826-6644); The Coupon Bank, San Diego (800-292-9250; in CA, 800-331-1076); the Flyer's Edge, Chicago (800-345-2525; 312-256-8200); the Coupon Broker, Denver (800-247-2891); Travel Mart, Dallas (800-443-CASH; in TX, 214-750-7600); International Air Coupon Exchange, Houston (800-558-0053 or 713-661-5234). These firms can conduct transactions by phone and they are also willing to purchase any mileage awards you may accumulate. Some dealers also buy and sell bumping vouchers (see p. 84).

TRADE-OFFS:
⊕ Mileage-Award Certificates ⊖

⊕	⊖
Substantial savings on first-class, business-class, and full-fare economy-class travel to most destinations	Little or no savings over discount fares
	Unsuitable for last-minute travel
Reserved seats on full-service airlines	Complicated ticketing procedures
	Some airlines aggressively cracking down on certificate brokering
	Tickets not valid for peak-period travel

AIRPORT TRANSPORTATION

It doesn't make sense to throw away the savings hard-won by thrifty pursuit of the perfect airfare on the ride in from the airport. Fortunately, you don't have to. Low-cost ground transportation options—sometimes a mind-boggling array of them—are available at most major airports. As usual, the more flexible your schedule, and the more inconvenience you can endure, the less you have to spend.

Taxis

There are basically three modes of ground transportation. *Taxis* take you exactly where you want to go exactly when you want to go there but are usually the most expensive. Comfortable and private, they are also always available either standing at the airport or on call. Some taxi drivers are local color incarnate; others, however, are cheats. To prevent the cheats from taking you on too much of a ride, if you are a stranger in town it behooves you to learn something about the route from the airport to your destination.

Since cabs usually charge per cab rather than per rider, they can be cheaper than limos for two or more people traveling together. Airport cab stands are great places to meet instant traveling companions. Several people traveling together can occasionally save money by sharing the cost of the private limousines that cruise many airports.

Airport Limos

Limo is the somewhat grandiose term for the privately operated buses and minivans linking airport to city. Limos generally cost less than taxis but they run on schedules to specific destinations, usually the major downtown hotels or a midtown bus terminal. Limos have comfortable seats, and luggage compartments inside and/or outside the vehicle. Limos often follow abbreviated schedules on weekend and off-peak hours, and seldom operate twenty-four hours.

Public Transit

Public transit—buses or subways—is invariably the cheapest way to go. Geared more for people who work at the airport than for travelers, these conveyances are part of the metropolitan public transportation network and, as such, differ widely in terms of comfort, convenience, and reliability.

For example, you can use public transportation to reach any point in New York City from LaGuardia or Kennedy airports for $2 (from Newark Airport, less than $3). But you will ride uncomfortable buses unequipped to carry baggage, negotiate circuitous routes through bleak outback neighborhoods, and make lengthy on-foot connections between the bus and the subway, and only then confront the dread New York City subway system itself. The trek to Midtown Manhattan from LaGuardia takes nearly an hour; from JFK, at least an hour and a half.

In Chicago, however, a clean new subway line that terminates within the O'Hare Airport terminal will take you to the Loop in half an hour for $.90; for a dime more you can connect with the entire Chicago bus system. And in Seattle, for $.85 peak/$1 off-peak, a clean and comfortable articulated bus makes regular runs from the airport to the heart of the downtown area.

Public transportation is cheap and, at least during peak hours, frequent. But since it is not normally geared for travelers, it does not offer express service to the most popular visitor destinations and lacks the apparatus for carrying luggage. Here's an instance in which traveling cheap can be equated with traveling light: Anyone encumbered with a great deal of baggage should avoid public transit.

Airport to the City

How do you find out about the ground transportation options available in each city? Most airports have conspicuously placed information desks that dispense directions and timetables. But it is difficult to impossible to find out much about ground transportation *before* you arrive unless you get a copy of Norman Crampton's *How To Get From The Airport to the City All Around The World*, a pocket-size volume that has become the Bible of the airport transportation scene.

The 1988–89 edition of *Airport to the City* contains information on all ground-transportation options (taxi, limo, public transit) for more than 350 airports in over 75 countries worldwide, including all major U.S. destinations. But *Airport to the City* does more than dispassionately list options. It describes and analyzes them and, where appropriate, designates the most time- and cost-effective mode of transit.

For taxis, *Airport to the City* includes international tipping customs and briefings on riders' rights. For limos, it lists fares, schedules, and stopping points. For public transit (toward which the author is unabashedly partial), the guide provides fares and schedules, stopping points, and directions for finding the right subway or bus.

Along with information, *Airport to the City* tosses off the odd cultural insight. For Venice it lists the prices and protocol for using water buses and taxis. In Seoul, travelers are warned to "beware of pickpockets on public buses and while waiting for them." It notes that "people often compare Budapest to Paris for charm and culture. Transit should be added to the list." And the Zurich listing rhetorically asks, "Where else but in Switzerland would they design a luggage cart that's *meant* to go with you on the escalator— by means of special teeth that hook into the escalator grooves? This is civilized traveling!"

My publisher, M. Evans and Company, has added *Airport to the City* to its line of *Cheap/Smart Guides*. It is available at bookstores nationwide, or you can order copies direct from the publisher. To receive a copy, send $4.95 (plus $1.00 postage and handling) to: M. Evans and Company, 216 East 49th Street, New York, NY 10017.

Thomas Cook Guide

The *Thomas Cook Airports Guide* is the European counterpart to Crampton's. The 362-page directory includes detailed schedules for public transit, rail, and bus service to central cities and surrounding areas from 150 European and British airports. Published twice a year (May and November), the guide costs $15.95 (plus postage) from: Forsyth Travel Library, P.O. Box 2975, 9154 W. 57th Street, Shawnee Mission, KS 66201-1375; or charge to Visa/MasterCard by calling 800-FORSYTH Monday through Saturday between 9:30 A.M. and 4:30 P.M. Central time.

Trains to the Planes

The cheapest and fastest way to get downtown from the airport usually turns out to be a subway or rail line. Because they are not impeded by highway congestion, subways are especially practical during rush hours. Subways and/or railroads serve most of the major European airports: London (Heathrow and Gatwick), Paris (Orly and DeGaulle), Amsterdam, Brussels, Dusseldorf, Frankfurt, Vienna, and Zurich. Outside of Europe, the only foreign facilities with rail service are Tokyo's Haneda and Narita airports.

A number of U.S. cities have subway service directly to the airport or nearby connections via special shuttle buses. Cities with subways all the way into the airport include Chicago, Philadelphia, and Cleveland. Those requiring shuttle connections include Boston, Oakland, and Washington-National (a short walk). At New York's JFK Airport a shuttle bus takes passengers to the JFK Express, a special—i.e., clean, secure, fast—subway service linking the airport to midtown for $6.50 one way (including free transfer to or from the regular subway system). Atlanta expects to extend a subway line to the airport sometime in 1988.

Airport to 'Burbs

While you can rely on Crampton's and other guidebooks for information to get you from the airport to the downtown area, it is extremely difficult to obtain accurate information about transportation from the airport to the suburbs or to nearby metropolitan areas. It's relatively easy to find out how to get to downtown Chicago from O'Hare, but how do you find out whether there are buses from the airport to Peoria, Illinois, Janesville, Wisconsin, or Kalamazoo, Michigan? (There are, to all three.)

Once you reach the airport, you can find out about transportation to outlying areas from the information desk in the terminal. But knowing in advance whether transit exists and when it operates helps you decide whether to rent a car, have someone meet you, and even when to fly.

Unfortunately, I can offer no handy rule-of-thumb-style solution. The ground transportation network at any airport consists of a hodgepodge of public transportation authorities, private limo and bus services, national bus lines, and taxi companies. Few airport authorities do anything to coordinate ground traffic. And there is seldom any single source for all information or even any place to call for referrals to ground transportation operators.

Fortunately, the situation is not entirely without hope. If you have access to a classified telephone directory for your destination, you can check for transportation to the suburbs or nearby cities under listings for "Airport Transportation," "Bus Lines," and "Limousine Service." Also, the latest edition of *Airport to the City* provides expanded coverage of suburban transit out of Dallas, Los Angeles, Chicago, New York, and other large cities.

The Port Authority in New York and New Jersey operates a phone service that provides information about ground transportation (bus, minibus, train, taxi, limo, or helicopter) from all three airports (LaGuardia, Kennedy, Newark) to the city as well as to suburban areas in New York, New Jersey, and Connecticut, and surrounding areas as far as Albany and Philadelphia. From the Eastern Seaboard between Massachusetts and Virginia, you can reach the service toll free Monday through Friday between 9:00 A.M. and 5:00 P.M. Eastern time at 800-AIR-RIDE (800-247-7433); from other areas you can call 212-466-7503.

On the West Coast, the California Department of Transportation publishes a comprehensive *California Airport Ground Transportation Directory* that details ground transportation options at twenty-three California airports. Along with complete information about cabs, limos, and bus service to surrounding communities, the directory lists hotel courtesy vans serving the airports. It is also updated annually; request a free copy from: Caltrans, Division of Aeronautics, P.O. Box 1499, Sacramento, CA 95807 (916-322-3090).

❝Avoid arriving at airports late at night when ground transportation options are sparse: Discount airfares that necessitate costly taxi rides to town may turn out to be no discount after all.❞

Airport-Bus Connections

Greyhound has service between 26 airports and cities within 250 miles. It now operates buses from the Portland, Maine, airport to the Maine towns of Augusta, Bangor, Brunswick, and Lewiston. From Newark, Greyhound operates service to Atlantic City, New Jersey; Hempstead, Huntington, Islip, on Long Island, New York; and Allentown, Bethlehem, Bristol, Easton, and Philadelphia in Pennsylvania. Greyhound also connects Phoenix, hub of the discount America West Airlines, to Flagstaff, Globe, Casa Grande, and Safford. Greyhound has no toll-free national number; for information about schedules you must call local numbers linked to the national system.

Some regional bus lines also provide direct airport connections to proximate cities. Peter Pan Lines (413-781-2900) connects Bradley Airport (Hartford) to Springfield, Holyoke, and Amherst (MA). Vermont Transit (802-864-6811) connects major destinations in Vermont and New Hampshire to Boston Logan Airport and the

SAMPLE NEW YORK TO LONDON AIRFARES, APRIL 15, 1988

RT = Round-trip travel required; AP = Advance-purchase requirement; L = Length-of-stay requirements; P = Penalty for cancellations and flight changes. Unless stated, service is from New York (JFK) to London (Heathrow); British Caledonian (BCal) uses London (Gatwick) Airport

AIRLINE/TRAVEL DEALER CLASS OF SERVICE	ONE-WAY FARE	RT	AP	L	P	CONDITIONS
British Airways Concorde	2999	No	No	No	No	Supersonic 3½ hour-flight (compared with 6½ on 747s); super deluxe meals; access to special airport lounges; no movie; helicopter to JFK
Pan Am, TWA, BA, BCal First Class	2280	No	No	No	No	Deluxe meal service; wide sleeper seats; drinks, headphones, gifts; airport lounge; helicopter to JFK
Pan Am, TWA, BA, BCal Business Class	1162	No	No	No	No	Deluxe reclining seats; deluxe meals, free drinks, in-flight entertainment, gifts; helicopter to JFK
Virgin Atlantic Upper Class	1162	No	No	No	No	New York (Newark) to London (Gatwick); superior meal service; free drinks, headsets; helicopter to Newark; free economy ticket
Pan Am, TWA, BA, BCal Economy	431	No	No	No	No	Fare applicable F-Su. travel; M-Th. fare, $406

SAMPLE NEW YORK TO LONDON AIRFARES, APRIL 15, 1988

RT = Round-trip travel required; AP = Advance-purchase requirement; L = Length-of-stay requirement; P = Penalty for cancellations and flight changes. Unless stated, service is from New York (JFK) to London (Heathrow); British Caledonian (BCal) uses London (Gatwick) Airport

AIRLINE/TRAVEL DEALER CLASS OF SERVICE	ONE-WAY FARE	RT	AP	L	P	CONDITIONS
Icelandair Economy	431	No	No	No	No	Connection in Rekjavík; crowded DC-8 cabin; no in-flight entertainment; weekdays, $406 (see index under "Icelandair")
Virgin Atlantic Economy	379	No	No	No	Yes	New York (Newark) to London (Gatwick); full meal service; cash bar; headset charge; crowded cabins; cancellation penalty increases toward departure date; weekdays, $349 (see index for "Low-Fare Carriers")
Continental Economy	375	No	No	No	No	Unrestricted coach service between New York (Newark) and London (Gatwick)
Pan Am, TWA, BA, BCal APEX Economy	352	Yes	21 days	7 days – 6 mos	Yes	Applies to half roundtrip F-Su.; M-Th. half roundtrips cost $327 (See index for "APEX fares")

Virgin Atlantic Economy	264	No	21 days	No	$50	Must be ticketed 21 days before departure or 14 days after booking, whichever comes first; $239 weekdays
Continental Economy	323	Yes	21 days	Yes	Yes	Applies to half roundtrip from New York (Newark) to London (Gatwick) on F-Su.; M-Th. half roundtrips, $298
Council Charter	249	No	No	No	$50	Charter service on Pan Am; round trips for $418-$438 depending on date of return (see index for "Charter Flights")
Kuwait Airways Economy From Maharaja Travel, New York	248	No	No	No	Yes	No charge cards; cancellation fee varies (see index for "Off-Price Dealers")
Virgin Atlantic Same-Day Saver	219	No	No	No	No	Must be booked on day of departure
Now Voyager Courier Agent	150	No	Yes	No	Yes	Free-lance air courier service using various scheduled carriers; carry-on baggage only; very limited availability (see index for "Courier Services")
Access International	140	No	21 days	No	$100	Tuesday-only flights on "major U.S. carrier" (see index for "Off-Price Dealers")

SAMPLE BOSTON TO LOS ANGELES AIRFARES, APRIL 15, 1988

RT = Round-trip travel required; AP = Advance-purchase requirement; L = Length-of-stay requirements; P = Penalty for cancellations, flight changes. All flights from Boston (Logan) to Los Angeles International

AIRLINE CLASS OF SERVICE	ONE-WAY FARE	RT	AP	L	P	CONDITIONS
American/United First Class	863	No	No	No	No	Nonstop service; deluxe seating and meal service; free drinks and in-flight entertainment
American/United Economy	575	No	No	No	No	Nonstop service; unrestricted
Continental First Class	495	No	No	No	No	Denver or Houston connection; deluxe seating and meals; free drinks, in-flight entertainment
American/Delta/Continental, etc. Economy	370	No	No	No	No	Connecting and multi-stop flights only

Continental First Class	244	Yes	7 days	Saturday night	25%	First-class excursion fare with one stop or Denver/Houston connection
American/Uniteddd Economy	189	Yes	7 days	Saturday night to 60 days	50%	Nonstop service; Tues., Wed., travel $169
American/United Economy	169	Yes	7 days	Saturday night to 60 days	100%	Connecting or direct (one or more stops) flights only; seats limited; Tues., Wed. travel, $149
American/United/Delta Continental, etc. Economy	159	Yes	7 days	Saturday night	100%	Connecting or direct (one or more stops) flights only; seats limited; Tues., Wed. travel, $139 (see index for "MaxSavers")

Burlington (VT) Airport. Bonanza (800-556-3815) provides service to Boston Logan from Providence and Newport, RI; Cape Cod, New Bedford, and Fall River, MA.

Capitol Trailways (717-233-7673) connects the Baltimore Airport (BWI) with Harrisburg, Scranton, Wilkes-Barre and Washington, D.C. Shortway North Star Lines (800-472-5540) serves Detroit Metro Airport from Toledo, Lansing, Grand Rapids, and points north. Evergreen Trailways (206-626-6090) has service between Seattle-Tacoma Airport and Victoria, British Columbia. For complete airport-bus connections, consult *Russell's Official National Motor Coach Guide* (see p. 108).

Transportation to and from the airport offers a multitude of opportunities to conserve travel dollars. Buses and subways are cheap but often slow, uncomfortable, and inconvenient. Limos are usually a reasonable alternative to costly taxis and slow public transportation; the best compromise is often a limo downtown and a cab to your destination.

―――――――――― ◈ TRAVELER'S ALERT ◈ ――――――――――

Ground-transportation options diminish during off hours. Public transportation seldom operates late at night and many limo services offer infrequent service or no service at all in the wee hours (in New York, for example, no limos or subways leave LaGuardia or JFK between 12:30 A.M. and 5:30 A.M.). At such times, arriving passengers have no alternative to costly taxis, and they may be lucky to find one of these. Take this into account when making travel plans: A discount flight that arrives when there is no alternative to a $25 cab ride to town may not be much of a discount after all.

FOUR

GROUND TRANSPORTATION

BUS TRAVEL: LEAVING THE DRIVING TO THEM

Many of us last encountered intercity buses during our days as impoverished students, when "travel" was synonymous with ride boards, backpacks, and crashing on somebody's couch. Yet in this era of deregulated skies when the disparity between bus and airfares has diminished to the vanishing point, it often makes sound financial sense to leave the driving to *them*. "Them," of course, refers to Greyhound, which, since its 1987 takeover of Trailways, is the only bus company operating on a national basis. Many local bus companies still offer regional interstate service.

The Pluses of Buses

The bus is still the *cheapest* way to reach many destinations. Except on the most highly competitive air routes, the bus is usually the least expensive way to travel between two points. On short hops between small towns, a bus may be the only alternative to a costly flight on a commuter airline. A flight from Chicago to Champaign, Illinois, for example, costs $65 on the Continental Express affiliate, Britt Airways; Greyhound charges $20 for the same trip.

"Passengers over sixty-five qualify for discounts on virtually all interstate bus service and on regular Amtrak fares."

Because Greyhound has established a *maximum one-way fare* applicable to any domestic route, savings on long hauls can be dramatic. The maximum fare changes with the season. However, in recent years it has not exceeded $150, and during recent fare wars it has dropped as low as $99. Greyhound also charges a maximum fare of $59 to any destination with 30-day advance-purchase and $15 cancellation fee.

This maximum fare becomes an even better deal with the allowance of *unlimited stopovers en route*. Greyhound tickets have time limits, as low as seven to fourteen days on special fares but thirty days on regular tickets. Unlimited stopover privileges permit passengers to stay anywhere along the route for as long as they wish, provided they reach the final destination before the ticket's expiration date. To take advantage of unlimited stopover privileges, passengers must upon boarding inform the driver where they want to make a stopover. Instead of collecting the ticket, the driver will then endorse it and return it to the passenger.

A one-way San Francisco–New York ticket (which ranged from $59 to $149 at various times in 1986) would permit stopovers in Reno, Salt Lake City, Cheyenne, Chicago, Cleveland, Pittsburgh, and Philadelphia. A Miami–Los Angeles ticket gives you a month to visit Orlando, Tampa, New Orleans, Houston, San Antonio, El Paso, Tucson, and Phoenix. A flight plan including all those stops would cost a great deal more.

Greyhound also offers *discounts to certain categories of passengers.* Senior citizens (sixty-five or older) get 10 percent off standard fares. Members of the American Association of Retired Persons (AARP) receive between 12 and 15 percent off, and members of Mature Outlook receive Greyhound coupon books good for discounts of from 15 to 50 percent. Greyhound offers discounts of 15 percent to members of the American Legion and allows handicapped passengers to bring along escorts free of charge.

Along with economy, the bus offers *convenience.* Few fares require advance purchase. Reservations are neither accepted nor necessary. Just buy your ticket at least thirty minutes before departure and if the first section of a run fills up, another bus will be added. Passengers who show up at the bus station on time are virtually guaranteed a seat. (Like airlines, buses offer compensation to passengers who volunteer to be bumped.) Indeed, if you decide at the last minute to travel on a holiday weekend, the bus may be your only option at any price.

Greyhound has *terminals at the center of the city,* a location that eliminates the sly extra costs for transportation to the airport.

Unlike Amtrak, which operates only one train a day to many destinations, and less than daily service to others, Greyhound has *frequent service* between most of its destinations.

Nowadays the bus is literally the *only form of public transportation available to some areas.* Amtrak service has persistently diminished, and deregulation has cost some localities all of their commuter air service. Some fairly well-known localities—Boone, North Carolina; Taos, New Mexico; Cooperstown, New York, to name but a few—are accessible only by bus or private car.

"Regular Amtrak and interstate bus tickets allow unlimited free stopovers en route until the expiration date of the ticket."

Bus travel also allows you to enjoy the *scenery.* Although Greyhound inevitably chooses interstate highways over scenic back roads, sometimes picturesqueness is unavoidable—across the Rockies,

U.S. 1 between Miami and Key West, alongside the Blue Ridge Mountains in Virginia and Tennessee, for example. The right to ride at any time without reservation permits you to cover the duller parts of the countryside by night and use the bus seat as a sleeper.

Greyhound Gripes

Of course, bus travel has drawbacks that should neither be minimized nor overlooked.

The most flagrant drawback is *speed*, the lack thereof. Buses are hobbled by the 55–65 mile-per-hour speed limit every other vehicle ignores, and it costs them a lot of time. A flight between New York and Washington, for example, takes about an hour; Amtrak Metroliners make it in under three hours; the slower Amtraks do it in about three and a half hours—but nonstop buses take four hours and twenty minutes. The one-hour flight between Chicago and St. Louis takes about five hours by train and six by bus. A bicoastal New York–Los Angeles journey, about six hours by plane, takes nearly three full days by bus.

Buses also *lack creature comforts*. They have washrooms but not always water fountains. Seats recline, but they are seldom as large or widely spaced as those on most airliners. No armrest divides contiguous seats, and a true inequity arises when an oversize seatmate cannot be physically prevented from encroaching upon your turf.

Bus-terminal food is a must to avoid. Your best hope these days is that the bus station will have consigned its food operation to a fast-food franchise—McDonald's, Burger King, and Hardee's are frequent concessionaires. Otherwise you are at the mercy of outrageously overpriced and unappetizing bus-terminal cafeteria or, worse yet, a bank of vending machines and a microwave oven.

Also be aware that bus lines regard *scheduled meal stops* as opportunities to make up for time lost to late starts and other delays. It is not uncommon for two four-hour legs to be interrupted by only one ten-minute rest stop.

"Travel" Versus "Transportation"

But perhaps the most off-putting aspect of bus travel is the ambience of indigence that permeates the entire experience. Going by bus delineates the difference between "travel" and "transportation": Taking the bus is brute transportation. The mass-transit experience begins at the *bus terminal*, where the downtown location so convenient for passengers makes it equally convenient for the city's low life. Airports are often ridiculed for being bland and sterile; bus terminals should live so long.

Bus companies accept *charge cards* at some but not all locations. Where they are accepted, it often takes an unconscionably long time to process the transaction.

Ticket *lines and lines* for boarding buses are long and slow, and buses often seem rather cavalier about adhering to schedules and explaining delays. There seems to be a tacit agreement between passenger and carrier that for anyone traveling by bus, money— not time—is of the essence.

Bus Times They Are A-Changin'

The bus industry is going through some changes, few for the better as far as passengers are concerned. Even the hard-core bus clientele have apparently realized that airfares are sometimes lower than bus fares. And bus traffic has diminished—down to thirty-three million passengers in 1985 from fifty-four million in 1980. In the spring of 1986, Greyhound discontinued routes in New England, South Carolina, Georgia, Arizona, and New Mexico, and canceled all service (except for the Airport Express System) within the state of Maine. Further service cancellations are expected on the West Coast and in New England and the Great Lakes region. Greyhound also sub-divided itself into four regional units—Eastern Greyhound with headquarters in New York, Central Greyhound in Chicago, Southern Greyhound in Atlanta, and Western Greyhound in San Francisco. The de-centralization will implement the company's strategy to stress short-hops and routes to markets not served by airlines.

Greyhound is also waging a campaign to eliminate one of its main advantages over air transportation—the midcity terminal. Greyhound has already announced that it will close 35 of its 113 and shift operations to terminals in the boonies, usually in shopping centers or alongside interstate highways. The first victims include New Orleans, Kansas City, Norfolk, Miami, Albuquerque, Erie and Scranton, Pennsylvania; Charleston, South Carolina; Albany and Syracuse, New York; Youngstown and Toledo, Ohio; Vallejo, Redwood City, and Long Beach, California; and Spokane, Washington.

There is, however, some cause for optimism. From its monopolistic position as the only transcontinental bus carrier, Greyhound rightly views discount air service, Amtrak, and private cars as its principal competition. Consequently, Greyhound can be expected to meet this competition with improved efficiency in service, more comfortable buses, tolerable waiting rooms, and innovative airline-style promotional fares. If this happens, we can look forward to seeing bus travel relinquish its role as black sheep of the U.S. transportation system.

Bus-Survival Tactics

If you take the bus, there is a great deal you can do to make the trip go more smoothly. When traveling alone, choosing a seat becomes a major dilemma. Take a window seat and you get a view and a chance for solitude, but you also risk the company of a 300-pound seat hog. Take an aisle seat and renounce view and solitude for the chance to choose your own seatmate destiny.

If you decide to "go for it" and take the window seat, you can increase your chances of riding alone by practicing obnoxious resistance. Put your coat, flight bag, box lunch, or whatever, on the seat beside you. Clamp on a Walkman headset. If the bus is completely full, someone will undoubtedly ask you to move it out of the way; otherwise they will probably sit elsewhere. If you're stopping to pick up additional passengers at another stop, put your belongings all around you and pretend to be asleep; embarking passengers will at least look around for an empty seat before disturbing you. An adherent of the obnoxious-resistance dogma must have the will to believe that if the bus departs with one empty seat, that seat will be next to him or her. (This principle also applies to Amtrak and any other open-seating conveyance.)

Much of your happiness onboard the bus depends on what you carry on with you. (Carry a flight bag or day pack; stow serious baggage below.) Try to find a timetable so you know when, where, and how long the bus stops. Bring a road map to follow the progress of the journey. Books and magazines that have been accumulating for months can now be perused at leisure. Buses are great places for really concentrating on puzzles.

Walkman-style tape player/radios are so perfectly suited for on-the-bus entertainment (and for deterring gabby seatmates) they might have been called Busman. Bring lots of tapes because radio reception is seldom very good onboard. Due to interference by the bus itself, AM stations hardly come in at all, and FM stations come through only when the bus is near the transmitter.

Carry on food and drink, at least a container of water, and some emergency snacks. Do not assume that a bus station will provide edible food. Do not assume that you will have enough time during rest stops or between connections (passengers change buses several times on long hauls) to forage for food very far afield from the terminal. To make time for a decent meal break, you'll need to miss a connection. Check your bag in a storage locker and look around (due to unlimited stopover privileges, this creates no ticketing problems).

USA by Bus and Train by Gary Hawkins (Pantheon Books, $9.95) contains a wealth of useful information for long-haul bus and train riders. Along with showing readers the ropes about riding these conveyances, the book contains twenty-seven model bus and train itineraries and includes information about budget lodging, food, and attractions located in the vicinity of bus and rail terminals.

Russell's Official National Motor Coach Guide is a phone-book-sized monthly publication that includes schedules for every intercity bus line operating in North America. Since schedules don't change very often, one edition should stay reasonably valid for quite a while. Subscriptions cost $63.20/year plus $6 postage; single copies are $7.60 plus $.50 postage from: Russell's Guides, Inc., P.O. Box 278, Cedar Rapids, IA 52406 (319-364-6138).

Although the bus as a form of transportation has numerous drawbacks, it should not be dismissed out of hand. For short hauls (150 miles or less), it is often the cheapest and most convenient way to travel. For longer trips, it is an inexpensive way to get the flexibility necessary for a leisurely excursion. Bus travel isn't always pretty, but it's always cheap and it's always there when you need it.

Plane-Bus Connection

The Greyhound Airport Express System provides low-cost connections between twenty-eight major airports and smaller cities within a 250-mile radius. This arrangement allows passengers traveling to or from smaller towns access to the major airports from which they can fly on cut-rate air carriers or use deep discount fares. Previous alternatives were to drive, take a bus to a downtown terminal and then go out to the airport, or fly costly commuter carriers.

GREYHOUND AIRPORT EXPRESS SYSTEM

Airport	Destinations
Albuquerque	Las Vegas, Roswell, Santa Fe, Taos, NM
Atlanta	Columbus, LaGrange, Macon, GA; Auburn, Lanett, Montgomery, Opelika, Tuskegee, AL
Burlington, VT	Montreal; Barre, Montpelier, Rutland, VT; Plattsburgh, NY
Chicago-O'Hare	Elgin, Rockford, IL; Beloit, Janesville, Kenosha, Madison, Milwaukee, Racine, WI
Columbus, OH	Athens, OH; Parkersburg, WV
Indianapolis	Bedford, Bloomington, Martinsville, Terre Haute, IN
Jacksonville	Brunswick, Savannah, GA; St. Augustine, FL
Louisville	Fort Knox, Owensboro, KY

GREYHOUND AIRPORT EXPRESS SYSTEM

Airport	Destinations
Miami	Homestead, Key Largo, Key West, Marathon, Miami Beach, N. Miami Beach, Perrine, FL
Midland/Odessa	Abilene, Big Spring, Pecos, TX
Milwaukee	Appleton, Fond du Lac, Green Bay, Madison, Oshkosh, WI
Minneapolis-St. Paul	Duluth, St. Cloud, MN; Eau Claire, WI
New Orleans	Baton Rouge, Hammond, Lafayette, Opelousas, LA
Newark	Atlantic City, NJ; Allentown, Bethlehem, Bristol, Easton, Philadelphia, PA; Hempstead, L.I., Huntington, L.I., Islip, L.I., Queens Village, NY; State Road, DE
Oakland	Fresno, Merced, Modesto, Stockton, Tracy, CA
Omaha	Lincoln, NE; Sioux City, IA
Phoenix	Casa Grande, Globe, Safford, AZ
Portland, ME	Augusta, Bangor, Brunswick, Lewiston, Rockland, Waterville, ME
St. Louis	Columbia, Ft. Leonard Wood, Jefferson City, Rolla, MO
San Francisco	Fort Ord, Los Gatos, Monterey, Salinas, San Jose, Santa Cruz, Stockton, Sunnyvale, CA
San Jose	Fort Ord, Monterey, CA
Seattle/Tacoma	Everett, Fort Lewis, Mount Vernon, Olympia, WA
Spokane	Colfax, Rosalia, WA; Lewiston, Moscow, Pullman, ID
Syracuse	Binghamton, Canton, Cortland, Elmira, Ithaca, Potsdam, Watertown, NY
Tampa	Bradenton, Ft. Myers, Lakeland, Port Charlotte, St. Petersburg, Sarasota, Venice, Winter Haven, FL
Tucson	Douglas, Sierra Vista, AZ

Bus Passes

The Greyhound Ameripass is the North American equivalent of the Eurailpass. For a flat fare passengers receive unlimited travel on any bus route during a specified period. Ameripass holders can travel anywhere a bus goes in the United States and Canada.

The Ameripass costs $189 for seven days; $249 for fifteen days;

$349 for thirty days; and $12 for each additional day up to the number of days specified on the original pass. Active members of the military, retired military personnel, and their dependents receive 50 percent discounts.

The Ameripass permits a great amount of freedom. You can go where the spirit moves you, stay for as long as the flavor lasts, and hop the next bus out of town. You don't have to plan because you can't make reservations. You can double back to favorite places and even commute. And, as visitors to Europe quickly discover with the Eurailpass and trains, these passes transform buses into free hotel rooms on wheels.

Whether or not the Ameripass represents an extraordinary bargain depends on how you travel. If you like to wander footloose and fancy free—and have an immense appetite for bus travel—the Ameripass is for you.

If you're traveling point to point with only a few stopovers or side trips, you will probably do better with the standard fare. In recent years, the maximum normal fare between any two points has not exceeded $149—$40 less than the seven-day pass. The normal fare allows thirty days for a trip and permits unlimited stopovers en route. To travel from Los Angeles to Boston with a few stops along the way, you would do better with one-way tickets in each direction.

Pass Words

The Ameripass goes into effect on the first day it is used, not on the day of purchase. The period of use does not include the first day of travel so, in effect, the pass includes one extra free day. The Ameripass can be used only by the purchaser, and pass holders will occasionally be asked to provide identification.

Carry maps and every Greyhound schedule you can lay your hands on. Also carry food, drink, and plenty to read. Finally, for the sake of your own mental health and out of pity for fellow travelers, don't sleep on the bus more than two nights in a row.

RENT-A-CARS

Hard-and-fast rules for uncovering car-rental bargains cannot be decreed. Car-rental rates fluctuate considerably in response to essentially the same factors that influence airfares: seasonal demand, competition within the industry, and general economic conditions. Rates for the same company vary between cities and between locations within a city.

As with air travel, the car-rental industry is rife with sales, specials, and price wars; and as with air travel, no one can predict where these deals will surface or how long they will last. This chapter draws a road map of the U.S. automobile-rental industry and offers a consumer's-eye view of potential pitfalls involved in renting cars.

The U.S. automobile-rental industry has three "tiers," which I've labeled according to the location of their offices in relation to a city's major airport. These are Airport Renters, Off-Airport Renters, and Off-Off-Airport Renters.

Airport Renters

Airport renters (ARs) are the industry biggies—namely, Hertz, Avis, Budget, and National. They are so called because their counters are located within the terminals of virtually every major U.S. airport. ARs also have multiple nonairport offices in most localities. They operate twenty-four-hour toll-free reservation numbers and their rental offices are open early in the morning, late at night, and all day on weekends.

The advantages of using ARs include quality of vehicle, service, and convenience. They have plenty of vehicles available in every price range. Until recently, ARs almost always included unlimited free mileage on all rentals. Lately, however, they have begun imposing limits on some rentals, typically free 75 to 150 miles on weekday or weekend rentals and 700 to 1,500 free miles on weekly rentals; $.15 to $.35 is then charged for each additional mile.

ARs are new—they are usually sold before they reach 25,000 miles—clean, air conditioned, and in excellent running condition. You can rent a car in one location and pay a "drop charge" to leave it somewhere else. The drop charge is usually substantial but, like everything else, it is subject to seasonal variation and promotional specials.

AR's operate extensive service networks that can repair cars quickly or, if necessary, quickly replace them. They offer substantial discounts to corporations and organizations, as well as to participants of various airline frequent-flyer programs.

"Renting cars is cheaper on weekends; it's also cheaper to rent from locations away from the airport."

The disadvantage of these renters is price: They charge the highest rates. Some locations are operated as franchises that do not necessarily adhere to national rates, promotions, or service policies. However, the need to get their huge volume of vehicles on the road on weekends or during nonpeak periods often inspires Numbers 1 through 4 to offer specials competitive with the cheapest of the cheap.

Off-Airport Renters

Instead of leasing costly counter space inside the airport terminal, off-airport renters (OARs) locate their offices off airport property but normally within a mile or two of the terminal. To reach their offices you must call for a courtesy-car pickup as soon as you land. The main national firms in this category include Ajax, Alamo, American-International (A-I), Dollar, Enterprise, General, Payless, Snappy, Thrifty, Tropical and Value. All of these companies operate toll-free, though not necessarily twenty-four–hour reservation numbers (see appendix).

OARs operate nationally, but their penetration is not as comprehensive as the ARs'. You cannot assume that they have outlets everywhere, and they are unlikely to have multiple outlets in any locality. OAR vehicles are generally as new and in as good condition as those of major firms, but they are more likely to be manual shift and lack air conditioning. Some OARs still offer unlimited free mileage.

OARs have fewer cars in each price range and cannot guarantee the service or replacement efficiency the larger firms provide. Most OARs offer corporate rates and many participate in airline frequent-flyer programs.

As you may have surmised, the main reason for using OARs is price. They usually charge less than major firms in the same market, at least $10 to $20 a day less. By using OARs you get essentially the same vehicle for a lower price by sacrificing a few fringe amenities and riding a shuttle bus to their headquarters.

Off-Off Airport Renters

Off-off airport renters (OOAR) are not necessarily located anywhere near an airport. This tier is divided into two subcategories: nationally franchised used-car rental outfits like Rent-A-Wreck, Rent-A-Dent, and Ugly Duckling; and independent local firms that may not even bear lightheartedly disparaging names. OOAR cars are neither luxurious nor new—Rent-A-Wreck vehicles range from two to six years old—but they purport to be in good running order.

The major OOARs operate toll-free numbers and offer airport pickup. Local OOARs have no toll-free numbers and usually can be reached only during normal business hours. Whether franchise or independent, they generally have only one location and thus cannot be used for one-way rentals. With the smaller firms, vehicle service can also be a consideration.

Off-off dealers generally include some free mileage in daily or weekly rates but charge extra for additional miles. When ARs and OARs offered unlimited free mileage, this was a competitive disadvantage. Now that the larger firms have matched their mileage limitation policies, there is even more reason to consider a bottom-of-the-line renter.

Because of the condition of their vehicles and the location of their offices, OOAR rates are significantly lower than those of the other two tiers. Rent-A-Wreck rates average $15 to $20 per day, $95 to $130 per week. Since most of these independent dealers have no national affiliation, the easiest way to find them is to consult the classified telephone directory for your destination. If you let your fingers do the walking before you go, you can compare their rates with those of national firms and get directions to their office from the airport.

OOARs offer opportunities for serious savings but only under certain circumstances. The condition of the vehicles plus the unpredictability of service plus the mileage charge may make OOARs inadvisable for long trips. Also, the special weekend rates almost always offered by the ARs and OARs can negate much potential OOAR savings.

A Rent-A-Case-Study: Denver

What kind of rate differences are we talking about? Here's a comparison of daily and weekly car-rental rates available in Denver, a major city that receives many business travelers and vacationers throughout the year.

The rates quoted here are undiscounted rates for the cheapest car available from each dealer—usually an economy or subcompact—with stick shift if available. The car would be rented at the airport or at the location nearest the airport and returned to the same place. Rates do not include gas, taxes, or optional insurance. These rates apply to a weekday in Denver.

Note: Since car-rental rates are subject to perpetual change, these figures are for comparison and in no way indicate a general nationwide price differential between car-rental firms. (FM = free miles.)

Rates at Ugly Duckling and Cheap Heaps vary according to the vehicle's age and "aesthetics"—air conditioning, radios, body— and smaller, more economical cars tend to be more expensive. At Cheap Heaps you must choose between the time-and-mileage or unlimited-mileage rate when you pick up the vehicle; however, the proprietors point out that the "breaking point" above which the unlimited mileage rate becomes advantageous is forty-two miles. (Denver, incidentally, is a hotbed of droll rent-a-names. Other dealers include Rent-A-Heap, Cheap Skates, Cheap Heaps, Rent-A-Lemon, Rent Rex on Wheels, and Colonel Clinker.)

RENTING A CAR IN DENVER

	DAILY	WEEKLY
Airport Renters		
Hertz	$43.99 + 100 FM/day	$109 + 700 FM/week
Avis	40.88 + 100 FM/day	98 + 700 FM/week
National	52.00 + 100 FM/day	104 + 800 FM/week
Budget	37.99 + 100 FM/day	110 + 700 FM/week

(All firms charge $.30/mile for each additional mile.)

	DAILY	WEEKLY
Off Airport Renters		
Alamo	$25.99 unlimited FM	$78 unlimited FM
Payless	18.75 + 150 FM	69 + 1050 FM/week
Snappy	27.95 + 150 FM	139 + 1050 FM/week
Thrifty	25.99 + 150 FM	109 + 1050 FM/week
Tropical	26.95 unlimited FM	109 unlimited FM

(Where applicable, extra miles cost $.15–.25/mile.)

	DAILY	WEEKLY
Off-Off Airport Renters		
Ugly Duckling	$13.95 + 100 FM	$80 + 700 FM
Cheap Heaps	12.99 + $.12/mile	130 + 400 FM
	OR 19.99 unlimited FM	

(Ugly Duckling charges $.10/mile for additional mileage; Cheap Heaps charges $.12/mile.)

Cutting Rent-A-Costs

Within each rental-car tier, certain other rate-saving rules generally apply. It is generally cheaper to rent cars on weekends—which on rent-a-car industry calendars may extend from Thursday noon to Monday noon—than on weekdays. A notable exception is the New York metropolitan area, where the highest rates in the country remain more or less constant throughout the week. It is cheaper to rent in the city than at the airport. Smaller cars and those with manual transmissions usually rent for less.

Additional Rent-A-Factors

Insurance   The optional collision-damage waiver (CDW) adds between $6 and $9 a day ($42 and $72 a week) to car-rental tabs. Renters who take the optional CDW are not liable for any damage. Those who forego the CDW may, in the event of an accident, be liable for damage for which they may or may not have been responsible. Most car rental firms now hold renters responsible for all damage, up to the full value of the car.

The insurance policy on your own car may cover your liability but using it on rentals may raise your rates; check it out with your insurance agent. Some states are considering regulation of the CDW. Until they do, however, it is prudent to bite the bullet and spring for the CDW.

Some bank cards—usually premium Visa and MasterCard—now offer CDW coverage for up to $3,000 of damage on cars rented with their cards. Unfortunately, almost every car rental firm (which previously had held customers who refuse CDW coverage responsible for only the first $2,000–$3,000 of damage) now make drivers liable for up to the *full value of the car.* Under these circumstances, it's risky to use this well-intended charge-card enhancement and drive a rented car with less than total coverage. However, American Express reimburses Gold Card members for up to $15,000 worth of damage and Platinum Card members for up to $50,000.

The CDW rip-off has been challenged by consumer groups and state governments which claim that CDW is a form of insurance and that the premiums—which pro-rate to $2,500–$3,600 a year —should be regulated by the states. Rent-a-car firms contend that CDW somehow is not really insurance but merely an option available to customers. The matter rests with the courts.

In the meantime, there are few prudent alternatives to buying the CDW. Some car renters—Value, Alamo—market packages that include CDW in the price of the rental. Members of General's

Executive Express Club get discount rates and a break on CDW. Membership is free and available to anyone; call 800-327-7607.

Even if you buy the CDW, other forms of rental car "optional" insurance (personal accident insurance, baggage insurance) are truly terrible deals and, assuming you carry health coverage, totally unnecessary. Car rental clerks try to dupe customers into buying them by asking if you want "the insurance" or wish to be "fully covered." Make it clear you want only the CDW. And when you sign the contract make sure that's all you're paying for.

Gas   Nobody includes gas anymore. Some firms start out rentals with full gas tanks and expect them to be full when the car comes back. Under these circumstances, you should keep your eyes open for cheap gas stations near the rental agency because they will top off your tank for prices only an oil sheikh could love. Other car renters promise that rentals start out with half a tank and charge accordingly—Alamo levies $11.50 for "½ tank minimum." Since you receive no credit whatsoever for gas returned with the car, your goal is to come as close as possible to coasting back to the lot.

Drop Charge   While it is usually a very high figure predicated upon mileage between the city at which you rent the car and the one in which you "drop" it, other factors may intervene. Sometimes a desire to shift inventory from one location to another will cause firms to cut or eliminate the drop charge. Major car-rental firms in Florida traditionally impose no drop charge between locations within the state.

Also, ARs occasionally offer no-drop-charge deals. National recently rented their cars at $10 extra per day with no drop charge between most locations. Although using a no-drop-charge deal may make you ineligible for other discounts, it is definitely worth investigating as an alternative to flying.

Charge Cards   Most car renters insist that customers have charge cards for security and identification—even if they intend to pay for the rental in cash. Other firms will make alternative arrangements to help you prequalify for a car. If you don't have a charge card, ask about the firm's policy when you call for a reservation.

Discount Rates   Almost anyone can qualify for discounts of 10 to 25 percent off regular rates. All of the employees of your firm may qualify. Members of professional associations or service clubs may qualify. Senior citizens or members of the American Association of Retired People may qualify. Barring that, participants in airline frequent-flyer clubs (see page 97) are entitled to discounts. Many airlines and car-rental firms have fly-drive packages offering free rental days or deep discounts. Ask either party—the airline or car renter—if such arrangements exist.

Seasonal Repositioning Freebies

There are certain occasions when you can drive rent-a-cars for free. These occasions occur when you happen to be going where the car renters want their cars to go at the time they want them to go there. Because car renters need to "seasonally reposition" vehicles where the customers are, this migration mimics the flight patterns of the Eastern Seaboard snowbird: south from the Northeast Corridor megalopolis to South Florida in fall and back north in spring.

Seasonal repositioning deals vary from year to year (and in some years are not available at all). In 1984-85, Avis gave customers a week to drive from Florida to any of the major airports in the Northeast Corridor plus Buffalo, Atlanta, or Houston. The deal cost $99 and included two Eastern Airlines tickets back to Florida. In 1985-86, National had 2,500 free cars driven from the New York area and Boston to six airports in South Florida. Drivers had ten days and 2,500 miles in which to complete the trip (after which standard rental rates were imposed) and paid only for gas and optional insurance.

No one knows what deals will be available in the future. This depends on such factors as the amount of seasonal business and the availability of vehicles. If you are interested in driving the Snowbird Trail in the autumn or spring, keep your eyes open for ads in local newspapers, or call a local office of one of the major rental firms.

◈ TRAVELER'S ALERT ◈

Car-rental rates are volatile, and no price uniformity exists among renters between cities or between the same renter's locations within a city. It pays to comparison shop, a practice that, due to the ubiquity of toll-free numbers, won't even cost you the price of a local phone call. Along with rates, check the price of collision-damage waivers and the gas policies, charges that often range high enough to rank as "deal points." Find out whether you qualify for a discount. And never consider the reservation made until the reservationist has given you a *confirmation number*, a precaution that helps to ensure that what you *hear* is what you *get*.

AUTO DELIVERY

See the U.S.A. in somebody else's Chevrolet! Or Ford, or Cadillac, or Toyota. Delivering cars for automobile-transport companies permits you to drive a late-model car for free to destinations all over the country. You won't enjoy the same freedom you would if you rented a car or drove your own, but for several people traveling together, it offers an opportunity for potent savings.

The Auto-Transport Industry

The business of auto-transport firms is arranging to have cars driven from one place to another. Their clients include corporations repositioning company-owned vehicles; banks receiving repossessed cars; auto dealers transferring used cars to areas where they will command higher prices (I once drove a two-year-old Olds Cutlass—loaded—from Milwaukee to New York where, I was told, it could be sold for $2,000 more); and private individuals who don't want to drive themselves.

Auto transporters charge clients according to the mileage covered, with prices ranging from about $150 for short deliveries to nearly $300 for the longest transcontinental routes. For their fee, transporters expedite all the paperwork, arrange for insurance, and obtain a "qualified driver"—you.

Auto-transport companies are easy to find in every city where they exist. They advertise profusely in the classified section of local newspapers under "Transportation" or "Travel." In classified telephone directories they are listed under "Automobile Transporters" or "Driveaway Companies." The largest firms with the most nationwide offices are Auto Driveaway, AACON Auto Transport, Auto Caravan and Transporters, Inc. After you decide when and where you want to travel, don't hesitate to contact all of the firms listed for your locality.

Driver Qualifications

Although qualifications vary somewhat among firms, all transport firms require a driver to be over twenty-one and have a valid driver's license from any state or country. Potential drivers for Auto Driveaway, the largest auto-delivery outfit, fill out applications asking for a physical description, employment history, personal references, a photograph, and fingerprints. References are checked but, for the most part, if you haven't made the firm's "bad list"—drivers with whom they have had trouble in the past —you will be able to drive.

Auto-transport firms require drivers to put up a deposit, in cash or traveler's checks, of from $50 to $150; the amount varies among firms and according to the length of the trip. Besides establishing a minimal degree of solvency, the deposit serves as a fund from which deductions can be taken in the event of driver infraction. Some firms accept a charge-card imprint in lieu of cash.

Drive Time

Drivers generally begin journeys with a full tank of gas; after that they are on their own. Higher gas allowances are occasionally offered on rush orders, so it is worth asking whether any of these are available. Cars are invariably new or nearly new and in excellent condition (Auto Driveaway imposes a $50 surcharge to deliver cars over six years old). More often than not, a car that someone is paying to have delivered is a top-of-the-line vehicle, fully equipped and in excellent running order.

Auto-transport firms impose both time and mileage limitations on their drivers. Time limits are reasonably generous. Auto Driveaway allows four days (not including the day on which the car is picked up) for deliveries from New York to Miami; nine days for Los Angeles to New York. That works out to about 400 miles of driving per day, or about seven and a half hours on the road at the fifty-five mile an hour national speed limit. Miss a deadline after alerting either the auto-transport firm or car owner and you may lose part of your deposit. Miss a deadline without alerting anyone and the car will be reported as stolen.

Mileage allowances are predicated on figures in the *Household Goods Carriers Bureau Agent Mileage Guide,* a monster tome that lists the most direct mileage between every two points in North America. Auto-transport firms usually pad that figure by about 10 percent, enough to get off the highway to find restaurants and motels but hardly enough for major diversions. If you exceed the mileage allowance, a per-mile charge (usually about $.25/mile) is deducted from the deposit.

If the car needs spot repairs, drivers will be reimbursed up to a certain amount, usually $50, when they deliver the car. More expensive repairs require authorization and forwarding of funds by the transport firm or car owner. Most firms supply drivers with an "accident packet" containing detailed instructions about what to do in the event of an accident. Larger firms supply drivers with toll-free numbers of lawyers in the home office.

On delivery, the agency, bank, car dealership, or private owner inspects the vehicle for damage. After the car passes inspection, the driver receives his deposit on the spot, either cash or a check cashable at a local bank. Also, it is not unknown for private owners, thankful at seeing their vehicle delivered in one unmolested piece, to sweeten the deal with generous tips.

For Flexible Travelers Only

One drawback of the auto-delivery deal is that you cannot make arrangements very far in advance. Transporters report that it is useless to call much earlier than three or four days before a pre-ferred departure date. Until then, they simply don't know whether they have the cars. Once the transport firm has a car, it will accept a partial deposit or about $25 and, barring unforeseen circum-stances, guarantee that the driver will travel on the day of choice.

On the other hand, auto delivery is great for last-minute de-cisions. If transporters have the cars, they want to move them ASAP. Call when the spirit moves you, and you may be on the road within hours.

Seasonal Trends

Although you can't make definite plans too far in advance, you can rely on certain seasonal trends in the auto-transport business. Auto Driveaway reports that during the "snowbird season" (Sep-tember to February heading south; February to May going north), cars are always available between the northeastern states and Flor-ida. It is also fairly easy to get cars going between New York and California throughout the year. If you're planning a trip where you drive one way and fly the other, note that the higher price for used cars in the Northeast attracts cars from all over the Midwest and the South. In other words, it is easier to get a car going toward the Northeast than away from it.

Travelers on the most leisurely and flexible itineraries can ad-vantageously use auto delivery on a step-by-step basis. A driver can, for example, pick up a vehicle in San Francisco, deliver it to Denver, and stay in Denver until he or she gets another car (with another full tank of gas, a $15 to $20 value) to drive to Chicago, where another car is picked up (and full tank) for the drive to Boston. Hard-core nomads can allow auto availability to plan their vacation. Wherever a car has to be delivered, that's where they go. It's hardly surprising that auto delivery is particularly popular among foreign visitors, who get to travel the United States in a fancy American car for only the comparatively low cost of gas.

Auto-Delivery Pros and Cons

Two or more people traveling together can save serious money by delivering cars; solitary travelers can't save very much at all. Consider a transcontinental trip from Washington to San Fran-cisco. Figure about 2,800 miles in a car that averages twenty-five miles per gallon of gas at $1.00 a gallon. That trip costs $112 for gas alone, not to mention tolls, motels, and road food. Since one-way airfare is less expensive, this does not represent much of a savings for solitaires. But with two or more people to divide the fixed costs and share the driving, the numbers look much better.

Drawbacks include the driver's inability to make definite plans very far in advance. Making plans even two weeks before you travel doesn't give you the absolute certainty that a car will be available. And cars are seldom available for short trips. For deliveries of less than 250 to 300 miles, transport firms generally use their own people.

Transport firms also make it clear that they have their eye on you; if you falter, you will be caught. And sometimes the people to whom you deliver the car cop an attitude, treating you as if you were some kind of a mooch whose status falls somewhere between hitchhiker and panhandler. The "dignity factor" is an issue here: auto delivery is not for the terminally pompous.

But transporting cars is a way for virtually anyone to travel extremely cheaply between most major destinations and a lot of minor ones. If you have the time for a road trip and enough flexibility to accommodate the uncertainty and possible slipups, transporting cars is the closest thing to a free ride.

AMTRAK BARGAINS

If buying air travel is a trip to a flea market, shopping for a train ticket is a visit to a state liquor store. All long-distance interstate trains are operated by the government-subsidized National Railroad Passenger Corporation, better known as Amtrak. Amtrak charges the mileage-based fares the airlines have been trying to reestablish for years. With few exceptions, the farther you travel, the more the ticket costs.

"Passengers over sixty-five qualify for discounts on virtually all interstate bus service and on regular Amtrak fares."

Although Amtrak fares seldom represent a savings over Ultra-Saver airfares or discount airlines, they do offer several cost-saving ways to enhance the joys of train travel.

Excursion Fares

Although Amtrak runs frequent specials, the principal permanent type of discount available to any passenger on every train (Washington–New York Metroliners are exceptions) is the round-trip excursion fare, which is between 110 and 150 percent of the one-way coach fare. These fares have no advance-purchase requirements but are subject to time limits of thirty or forty days, stopover limitations, and blackout periods.

All Aboard America

The *All Aboard America* discount program was introduced as a limited-time promotion but appears to have become an Amtrak fixture. Basically, the program divides the United States into three regions with imaginary lines between Wolf Point, Montana–Denver–Albuquerque–El Paso and between Chicago–Memphis–New Orleans. Round-trip train fare is $138–$159 (depending on time of year, higher during summer) or less for travel between any two cities located within a region; $188–$239 between points in adjoining regions; and $238–$299 for travel covering all three regions.

All Aboard America fares have no advance-purchase requirements, and three stops—a final destination and one stopover in each direction—are permitted. These fares are not valid when purchasing sleeping accommodations in some peak periods. Reservations and tickets for the entire journey must be obtained before departure, and all travel must be completed within forty-five days of the first day of travel. For shorter trips, Amtrak has a *$7 Return Fare*. Whenever the one-way fare exceeds $60 (with no change of trains), the return trip costs only $7 more.

Low-Cost Compartments

Passengers on eastern Amtrak routes can occupy a slumber coach—a private compartment equipped with day seats, fold-down beds, and a cunning fold-out washroom—for considerably less than the price of bedrooms and roomettes. The slumber coach between New York and Chicago costs $34 for one passenger, $59 for two (plus regular coach or excursion fares); a one-person roomette on the same route costs $119, and a two-person bedroom is $218.

Slumber-coach facilities are available only on certain eastern trains: the Lake Shore Limited and Broadway Limited between New York and Chicago; the Montrealer between Washington and Montreal; the Silver Meteor and Silver Star between New York and Miami; and the Crescent between New York and Atlanta.

The best discount-compartment deals in the West are economy bedrooms. They run about half the price of standard bedrooms but lack private baths. Between Chicago and Los Angeles, an economy bedroom costs $186 (plus the regular fare) for one or two passengers, compared with $405 for a deluxe bedroom equipped with a bathroom and shower. Spacious family bedrooms, which sleep four and extend the width of bilevel cars, have windows on both sides, but no bathroom, and cost $285 on the Chicago–Los Angeles run. Economy and family bedrooms are available on most of the long-haul trains operating in the West: the Southwest Chief and Desert Wind between Chicago and Los Angeles; the Eagle between Chicago and San Antonio; the Sunset Limited between New Orleans and Los Angeles; the California Zephyr between Chicago and Oakland; and the Pioneer between Chicago and Seattle.

Categorical Discounts

Amtrak also offers particular categories of travelers a number of discounts off regular fares. On the *Family Plan,* one adult pays the full one-way or round-trip fare; the spouse and children between twelve and twenty-one get 50 percent off; and children between two and eleven get 75 percent off. Children between two and eleven get a 50 percent discount when accompanied by an adult of eighteen or older. Since Family Fares are not subject to excursion fare blackout restrictions (11 A.M.–8 P.M. Friday and Sunday), they are especially valuable for peak-period travel and one-way trips.

Senior citizens (sixty-five and older) and *handicapped* travelers get 25 percent off one-way and round-trip travel except during certain blackout periods. Soldiers on active duty or within seven days of discharge get 25 percent off the regular *military discount.*

Unfortunately, these discount programs cannot be combined with excursion fares. In some cases, notably the senior citizens and handicapped programs, which require round-trip travel, the regular excursion fare may turn out to be cheaper. In all events, compare excursion fares with the rates for applicable discounts.

Stopover Privileges

Amtrak stopover privileges do not necessarily save money, but they do offer a lot more for the travel dollar. Passengers with nondiscounted coach tickets between any two points can stop anywhere along the route and stay for as long as they wish provided they reach their final destination before the ticket expires. The one-way coach fare from Boston to San Francisco is $325, which is more than the MaxSaver fare on major airlines. However, Amtrak passengers can make stopovers in Albany, Syracuse, Rochester, Buffalo, Cleveland, Toledo, Chicago, Omaha, Denver, Salt Lake City, Reno, and Sacramento for no additional charge.

"Regular Amtrak and interstate bus tickets allow unlimited free stopovers en route until the expiration date of the ticket."

To take advantage of the liberal stopover privileges, you must have reservations on the trains you use. If you plan to make stopovers, Amtrak advises you to "ask your ticket or travel agent to provide separate coupons to and from the stopover point. If traveling in reserved coach, club car or sleeping car accommodations, make your initial reservation only to the point of stopover and then make separate reservations onward from that point. In the case of club or sleeping car accommodations, this will cause charges slightly higher than for passengers traveling through, since separate charges will apply to and from each stopover point."

Additional Ambargains

• Amtrak operates a nationwide twenty-four–hour toll-free reservation and information: 800-USA-RAIL (800-872-7245).

• Amtrak accepts major credit cards for the purchase of tickets and for meals on club cars and full-service dining cars.

• Amtrak provides uniformed redcaps for baggage assistance at most major stations. Their services are free, but tips (at least $.50 per bag) are appropriate. Avoid unauthorized baggage handlers, and make sure the redcap gives you a claim check for each piece of luggage.

FIVE

LODGING

BUDGET HOTEL/MOTEL CHAINS

The hotel industry defines "budget motel" as a property that charges between 20 and 40 percent less than a Holiday Inn or other standard hotels in the same area. Budget motels—"budgetels" for short—originally catered to families who wanted to sleep cheaply near an interstate highway. To attract the more cost-conscious segment of the business travel market, budgetels have recently expanded their domain to include large cities and airports. Today more than eighty budget-motel chains offer a total of more than 350,000 rooms.

Budgetels are truly inexpensive—as low as $18 a night in some locations and seldom more than $35. What you get for your money is a clean room with a bed, basic Motelroom Moderne furnishings, free parking, TV, usually a phone, and sometimes a pool. Budget motels usually compensate for the lack of restaurants, bars, sit-in lobbies, and room service with banks of well-stocked vending machines. Most of them have toll-free reservation numbers and nearly all—including, as of recently, Motel 6—accept charge cards.

The majority of budgetels are franchise operations. The franchiser—Motel 6, Red Roof Inn, Super 8, and others—mandates the basic standards of decor and service to which the franchisee —the owner of the individual motel—must comply. How closely these standards are met depends upon the integrity of the franchisee and the policing procedures of the franchiser.

Today budget hotels are located almost everywhere: along interstate highways, near airports, around major tourist destinations, and on the fringes of large cities. Probably the only kind of place you won't find them in is the central business district of major cities, areas increasingly limited to "the Ritz" or "the pits," and hardly anything in between.

The disadvantages of budgetels involve what you don't pay for and, consequently, don't get. Locations are seldom prime. They are rarely the motels closest to the airports or tourist attractions, and travelers without cars may not be able to reach them at all. Rooms seldom have views or much of anything else in the way of character, and the quality of service is determined by the owner.

Budgetels are easy to find. Every chain distributes a free directory of its properties. Call those with toll-free reservations numbers to request a copy; write away or pay for the call to the others. Here are some of the addresses and phone numbers of the major budget-motel chains. Prices indicate average national rates for single/double rooms.

Allstar Inns (2020 De La Vina, P.O. Box 3070, Santa Barbara, CA 93130-3070 805-687-3383). Incorporating *Western 6* and *California 6*, Allstar Inns includes more than 130 properties in the Southwest and along the West Coast. Call individual properties for reservation ($21–$26/$27–$30).

Budget Host Inns (P.O. Box 10656, Fort Worth, TX 76114; 800-835-7427). Budget Host Inns is a referral service for more than 225 independent motels in thirty-seven states and British Columbia. Most of its affiliates are located in the Midwest and Southwest. There is a toll-free number, but guests receive a $1 rebate if they pay for the call. The directory contains bonus coupons ($18–$36/$20–$50).

Comfort Inn (10750 Columbia Pike, Silver Springs, MD 20901; 800-228-5150). The 400-property budget division of Quality Inn has properties all over the country, Europe, and Canada ($18–$45/$22–$55).

EconoLodge (P.O. Box 240066, Charlotte, NC 28224-0066; 800-446-6900). This chain has more than 400 properties in 36 states, but the majority of them are located east of the Mississippi. There is a seventh-night free program ($20–$40/$25–$45).

Exel Inn (4706 East Washington Avenue, Madison, WI 53704; 800-356-8013; in WI, 800-362-5478). There are almost thirty properties in the upper Midwest and in Texas. An "insider's card" thirteenth-night free discount is offered ($22–$38/$27–$43).

Friendship Inns (2627 Paterson Plank Road, N. Bergen, NJ 07047; 800-453-4511). This is an affiliation of 107 independent motels located in the United States and Canada. Properties can be found in almost every state ($17–$68/$20–$70).

Hampton Inn (6799 Great Oaks Road, Suite 100, Memphis, TN 38138; 800-HAMPTON, Monday through Friday, 7:00 A.M. to 7:00 P.M. Central time). The budget division of Holiday Inn itself, Hampton Inn currently has more than 160 properties distributed throughout the country, and there are more on the way ($28–$53/$32–$60).

Hospitality International (1152 Spring Street, Suite A, Atlanta, GA 30309; 800-251-1962). This company has three budget-motel chains—*Scottish Inns, Red Carpet Inn,* and *Master Hosts Inns* —with 181 units in twenty-three states and Canada. They tend to be concentrated in the South ($20–$40/$25–$50).

BUDGET MOTEL CHAINS

NAME & ADDRESS	RES. NO	NO. UNITS	LOCATION	RATES	NOTES
Allstar Inns 2020 De La Vina P.O. Box 3070 Santa Barbara, CA 93130-3070	805-687-3383	133	Southwest West Coast	S: $21–$26 D: $27–$30	Incorporates Western 6 and Allstar Inns; call individual units for reservations
Budget Host Inns P.O. Box 10656 Forth Worth, TX 76114	800-835-7427	225	Midwest Southwest British Columbia	S: $16–$36 D: $22–$50	Referral service for 200 independent motels; directory contains bonus coupons
Comfort Inn 10750 Columbia Pike Silver Spring, MD 20901	800-228-5150	400	Nationwide, Canada, and Europe	S: $18–$45 D: $22–$55	Budget division of Quality Inn
EconoLodge P.O. Box 2400066 Charlotte, NC 28224-0066	800-446-6900	400	36 states but most east of Mississippi	S: $20–$40 D: $25–$45	7th night free program
Exel Inn 4706 East Washington Ave. Madison, WI 53704	800-356-8013 In WI: 800-362-5478	30	Midwest Texas	S: $22–$38 D: $27–$43	Insider's card 13th night free program

BUDGET MOTEL CHAINS

NAME & ADDRESS	RES. NO	NO. UNITS	LOCATION	RATES	NOTES
Friendship Inns 2627 Paterson Plank Road No. Bergen, NJ 07047	800-453-4511	107	United States, Canada	S: $17–$68 D: $20–$70	An affiliation of independent motels in almost every state
Hampton Inn 6799 Great Oaks Road Suite 100 Memphis, TN 38138	800-HAMPTON	160	Evenly distributed around United States	S: $28–$53 D: $32–$60	Budget division of Holiday Inn; nonsmoking rooms, free continental breakfast, free local phone calls
Hospitality International 1152 Spring Street Suite A Atlanta, GA 30309	800-251-1962	181	23 states but concentrated in South	S: $20–$40 D: $25–$50	Incorporates three budget chains: Scottish Inns, Red Carpet Inn, and Master Hosts Inns
Imperial Inn 100 Wilson Blvd. Suite 820 Alexandria, VA 22209	800-368-4400 In VA, 800-572-2200	125	Nationwide with concentration in Far West	S: $20–$45 D: $22–$55	Special rates for business people, seniors, and the military

Name / Address	Phone	Number	Area Covered	Rates	Notes
Knights Inn 6561 E. Livingston Ave. Reynoldsburg, OH 43068	—	90	The Midwest, South, and Florida	S: $28–$38 D: $34–$43	Write for directory and call collect for reservations; kitchenettes; non-smoker rooms
Mc Sleep Inn 10750 Columbia Pike Silver Spring, MD 20901	800-MC-SLEEP	20	Nationwide	S: $20–$29 D: $20–$29	New Quality International budget line plans to open 200–300 motels by early 1990s
Motel 6 51 Hitchcock Way Santa Barbara, CA 93105	505-891-6161	400	39 states but concentrated in California, the Northwest, and Texas	S: $17–$20 D: $21–$24	Motel 6 now has free TV, free local phone calls, and a nationwide reservation number; most charge cards accepted
Red Roof Inns 4355 Davidson Road Hilliard, OH 43026-9699	800-848-7878	175	Mostly east of the Mississippi	S: $21–$32 D: $28–$35	Free ESPN, first-run movies, newspaper, and morning coffee
Regal 8 Inns P.O. Box 1268 Mt. Vernon, IL 62864	800-851-8888	50	Midwest West South	S: $22–$27 D: $26–$35	Free coffee, non-smoker rooms.

BUDGET MOTEL CHAINS

NAME & ADDRESS	RES. NO	NO. UNITS	LOCATION	RATES	NOTES
Super 8 **P.O. Box 4090** **Aberdeen, SD 57401**	800-843-1991	500+	45 states and Canada but mostly Midwest, Southwest, and Far West	S: $20–$52 D: $24–$68	
Susse Chalet **One Chalet Drive** **Wilton, NH 03086**	800-258-1980	37	Mainly New England	S: $32–$45 D: $36–$47	Discounts and privileges to members of VIP Club

Imperial Inn (1000 Wilson Blvd., Suite 820, Alexandria, VA 22209; 800-368-4400; in VA, 800-572-2200). There are about 125 properties scattered nationwide, with a concentration in the Far West ($20–$45/$22–$55).

Knights Inn (6561 E. Livingston Ave., Reynoldsburg, OH 43068; 614-866-1569). This is a ninety-unit chain concentrated in the Midwest, the South, and Florida. Nonsmoker rooms are available, as well as kitchenettes. Write for the directory, and call collect for reservations ($28–$38/$34–$43).

McSleep Inn, (10750 Columbia Pike, Silver Spring, MD 20901; 800-MC SLEEP). Quality International's new line of budget motels expects to open 200-300 properties nationwide by the early 1990s. ($20–$29/room).

Motel 6 (51 Hitchcock Way, Santa Barbara, CA 93105; 505-891-6161). This is the biggest—400 units in thirty-nine states—and the cheapest of the budget-motel chains. TV is now free, swimming pools are "almost always" available, and a phone system is currently being installed nationwide. They are located nationwide but are concentrated in California, the Northwest, and Texas ($17.95/$21.95; $25.95 family plan for up to four persons).

Red Roof Inns (4355 Davidson Road, Hilliard, OH 43026-9699; 800-848-7878). This chain is known as the "sleep cheap" people, with 175 units located largely east of the Mississippi. Free ESPN, first-run movies, newspaper, and morning coffee are standard features ($21–$32/$28–$35).

Regal 8 Inns (P.O. Box 1268, Mt. Vernon, IL 62864; 800-851-8888). More than fifty properties in the Midwest, West, and South offer free coffee, pools, non-smoker rooms. ($22–$27/$26–$35).

Super 8 (Attn: Marketing & Advertising Division, P.O. Box 4090, Aberdeen, SD 57401; 800-843-1991). There are more than 500 units in 45 states and Canada, the majority of which are located in the Midwest, Southwest, and Far West ($20–$52/$24–$68).

Susse Chalet (Chalet Drive, Wilton, NH 03086-0657; 800-258-1980). There are more than thirty-five motor lodges in this chain, many of which are luxurious. Almost all units are located in New England ($32–$45/$36–$47).

Budgetel Guidebooks

State-by-State Guide to Budget Motels by Loris G. Bree (MarLor Press) is a useful directory to low-priced chain and independent motels; $6.95 in stores, $7.50 from MarLor Press, 4304 Brigadoon Drive, St. Paul, MN 55112.

Rand McNally's *Lodging for Less* books are distillations of the Mobil Travel Guides listing assorted types of lodgings (hotels, motels, inns, cottages, resorts) that generally charge $37.50 or less for double rooms (higher-priced exceptions occur in locales where little or no "quality" lodgings exist at that price). The series now has three volumes—Northeast and Middle West, South, and West—and costs $4.95 per book.

The Y's Way

It is fitting to herewith note that the granddaddy of budget lodging—the YMCA—is alive and still quite well. The Y's Way International (the organization that handles reservations for the YMCA) runs 107 "lodging centers" in 57 North American cities and 19 foreign countries.

The main advantages of staying at a YMCA are the convenient downtown location and low price. Single rooms in North American Y's range from $8 to $27 a night (only Dallas and Washington exceed $30); doubles range from $20 to $44. And unlike the budget motels, which are mainly consigned to the boonies, YMCAs are usually located right in the heart of town.

A YMCA may represent the cheapest decent downtown accommodations available in pricey cities like New York (four locations with more than 2,000 rooms), Chicago, New Orleans, Boston, Philadelphia, Dallas, Houston, Washington, Detroit, San Francisco (three locations), Los Angeles, Toronto, Montreal, and Vancouver. Overseas Y's Way International lodging centers are located in most European countries as well as in Israel, Australia, New Zealand, Hong Kong, Japan, and Malaysia.

YMCAs are not invariably male only, nor do they always segregate the genders. Of the sixty-three in North America, twenty-one are for men only, seventeen house men and women in separate rooms, and twenty-five permit men and women to stay in the same room.

Y Not?

Though invariably clean and secure, YMCA accommodations generally cross the fine line separating no-frills from Spartan. You get a room, a bed, possibly a TV. You may or may not have a private bath, but most YMCAs have pools, sports facilities, libraries, and recreation rooms.

Doing It Y's Way

Reserving a room at the YMCA of your choice, however, is something of a hassle. A directory of Y's Way International properties can be obtained by sending a business-size (no. 10), self-addressed stamped envelope to: The Y's Way, 356 West 34th Street, New York, NY 10001. This brochure contains instructions for using the central computerized system to make reservations at any world-wide facility. It recommends making reservations and paying (by traveler's check, cashier's or certified check, or U.S. money order only) at least two months before arrival. Fees of $3 for each domestic center and $5 per international center are added to reservations made fewer than sixty days in advance.

If you don't have time to make an advance reservation through New York, try calling the specific Y directly. If they are among the few units that accept credit cards (most accept only cash or traveler's checks), they will accept prepaid reservations. In some cases, the New York office (212-760-5850/57/92/40) will make a last-minute reservation for you. Otherwise you can show up on their doorstep and hope there's room at the inn.

YMCAs are clean, safe, comfortable places in which to sleep (and eat) cheaply. They offer recreational and social facilities—they are particularly popular among young foreign visitors—but skimp on amenities and general creature comforts. Still, in cities like New York and Washington, where $50 hotel rooms are a bargain, the Y's Way may be your best way of avoiding "lodging poor" vacations.

CHEAP (BUT DECENT) DOWNTOWN HOTELS

Cheap-but-decent downtown hotels are among the Great American lodging bargains. Unfortunately, like a lot of Great American bargains, they are in the process of vanishing. These hotels may have been among the best places in town back when business-people were business*men* and all of them traveled by train. Many of them have made the renovations necessary to make them elegantly gracious evocations of a bygone era. Others have bitten the dust. However, an unchosen few have managed to survive—if not thrive—and exist today in a condition best characterized as arrested decay.

The hotels I refer to have convenient locations but physical plants too shabby to compete with refurbished grande dames or new Hyatts and Marriotts for the up-scale guest. Because they have managed to stay just above the fine line separating fleabag from flophouse, they represent conspicuous bargains.

Top Locations/Bargain-Basement Rates

The main advantages of staying in a cheap-but-decent downtown hotel are location and price. Built in the era of railroads, these hotels are inevitably located close to what is or was the central business district. Because they have fallen into disrepair, they charge much less than newer or better preserved hotels—often much less. It is not unusual to find a respectable hotel room in the downtown area of a major American city for less than $30. The rooms themselves are often more than what you paid for: larger, with better views, and furnished funkily enough to make Bogie himself feel right at home.

In addition to price and location, these hotels often have an ambience much closer to the spirit of the city. Milwaukee's Hotel Wisconsin vibrates with the footfalls of past generations of dairy-men and loggers. The Croyden evokes the wide-open Chicago of Prohibition days. The Edison in New York, The Essex in San Francisco, The Cadillac in Rochester, The Commodore in Seattle, and The Miles in Salt Lake City all take you back to another era.

The disadvantages of downtown hotels are furnishings (old and cheap), amenities (sparse), and service (indifferent to nonexistent). Beds may be intolerably soft, TVs black-and-white or among the missing, and carpeting frayed into transparency.

Sometimes these midtown survivors are not as clean as they might be, and you may not feel entirely comfortable sharing a slow-moving elevator with some of your fellow guests.

Also, the downtown location so primo by day may be less than desirable after dark when the city turns into a pumpkin. With movie theaters and most of the restaurants having long since mi-grated to distant neighborhoods and shopping malls, the downtown areas of many major U.S. cities—Dallas and Detroit among many others—are as lively as tombs.

Sleuthing Downtown Hotel Bargains

By far the biggest disadvantage of cheap-but-decent downtown hotels is that they're becoming increasingly hard to find. Sus-pended between renovator and wrecking ball, these hotels seldom have much to spend on advertising and promotion. Since many of the low-priced hotels are not listed in the *Red Book*, the annual directory of the American Hotel and Motel Association, travel agents couldn't find them even if they wanted to.

One source for cheap downtown hotels is the *classified telephone directory* for your destination. Consult it at a public library before you leave, or find one as soon as you reach your destination. These hotels often spring for display ads stating exactly what they are—inexpensive centrally located hotels. If the listing is vague about location, the address itself should hold some clue: Low numbers usually indicate midtown locations.

Some *tourist information services* provide excellent listings of hotels in every price range. Some of the better free directories include: *Hotels in New York City*, from the New York Convention and Visitors Bureau, 2 Columbus Circle, New York, NY 10019 (212-397-8250); *San Francisco Lodging Guide*, the San Francisco Convention and Visitors Bureau, P.O. Box 6977, San Francisco, CA 94101 (800-843-8000; 415-974-6900); and *Lodging*, the Seattle-King County Convention and Visitors Bureau, 1815 Seventh Avenue, Seattle, WA 98101 (206-447-4240).

Among national and international *guidebooks*, the *Let's Go* series published by the Harvard student agencies contains the most comprehensive coverage of the cheap downtown hotel genre. However, the guide cautions readers about following its advice. "*Let's Go* hasn't listed the most notorious hotels, but we've kept some of those on the borderline between the disagreeable and the disreputable." *Let's Go* advises travelers—especially single female travelers—to read their listings carefully and "take the normal precautions you would ordinarily take in a large city." It also suggests that travelers with cars might be better off at a budget motel on the outskirts of town.

The budget hotels listed in *Arthur Frommer* guidebooks tend to be slightly more up-scale than those in *Let's Go*. *Fodor's* guides include good listings of low-priced hotels, but, inexplicably, hotel phone numbers are omitted in both *Budget Travel in America* and *Fodor's U.S.A.* (Phone numbers are included in local budget guides.)

Reservation Services

Most European cities have services that will reserve hotel rooms in any price category conveniently located at airports, rail terminals, and other central locations. The closest comparable U.S. entity is a little-known outfit called Meegan Hotel Reservation Service, which books hotel rooms in any price range anywhere in the country. Located in New York City, Meegan operates reservation counters or courtesy phones in all three New York airports, Penn Station, the Port Authority Bus Terminal, and Logan Airport in Boston. Where it does not have desks or courtesy phones, Meegan can be reached at a twenty-four-hour toll-free number: 800-221-1235.

Although Meegan will book rooms in any hotel, it is most valuable for ferreting out cheap-but-decent small hotels in big cities. In pricey Manhattan, Meegan lists at least ten hotels with rooms for less than $35 a night and a few for as little as $25 (with shared bathrooms). Regardless of where you're going in the United States, call Meegan in advance or as soon as you arrive and discuss how much you want to spend. If a room in your price range exists, a reservation will either be made for you or you will be given the appropriate number to call.

In the Washington, D.C., area, the Washington Central Reservation Center (800-554-2220) provides visitor information and makes reservations at hotels in every price range. Although cheaper lodgings may be found in the suburbs, the Center says a double room in the meanest downtown Washington hotel costs $50 and upwards. Because of bulk booking, the Center sometimes obtains lower rates than individuals. If you make an advance reservation (eight weeks in advance for peak March–May and September–November seasons is suggested), you will receive a written verification and map indicating the hotel. Otherwise, call anytime and they will find some place for you.

The Washington Central Reservation Center has affiliated services for Orlando (800-322-2220) and Hilton Head Island (800-845-7018). Centralized toll-free reservation services also operate for the state of Maryland (800-654-9303; in MD, 800-695-9304) and Key West, Florida (800-327-4831; in FL, 800-356-3567).

◊ TRAVELER'S ALERT ◊

Taking the cheap-hotel route involves some risk, but there are ways to protect your posterior. Try to have at least two listings for every city you visit: If the first is totally uninhabitable, you still have somewhere to turn.

Often these hotels have gone to seed because only a portion of the rooms are too noisy, small, stuffy, or disheveled for human occupancy. Make sure you don't get stuck with one of these by asking to inspect your room before you check in. If the hotel won't let you, walk.

And if every place you turn seems too "atmospheric" for even your adventurous proclivities, don't be ashamed to cut and run to the nearest Ramada.

HAGGLING FOR HOTEL ROOMS

❝Hotel rooms are unregulated commodities subject to the volatile effects of supply and demand: Feel free to negotiate a lower rate.❞

Like airline tickets, hotel rooms are perishable commodities. An empty seat on a departed plane is worth exactly as much as an empty bed the morning after—zilch. Unlike airline tickets, however, hotel rooms are seldom subject to governmental regulation, adhere to no official published rates, and comply with the pricing policies of no international cartel. Management sets hotel rates, and management has the prerogative to slash them at will.

Dialing for Deals

When you call a hotel or a hotel chain toll-free reservation service to make a reservation, ask for the lowest rate available during the time you want to stay. If you don't ask for the lowest rate, they may quote you something higher. That establishes a minimum regular rate. If your stay will include a Friday, Saturday and, in some cases Sunday, find out if the hotel offers any weekend deals. If not, ask if any other specials apply to that period.

You often find a better deal if you bypass the toll-free national reservations operator and buy a phone call directly to the hotel. National operators may not be aware of local promotions. And they certainly lack the authority to negotiate room rates with customers. The toll-free operators can provide the hotel's local number—and save you Ma Bell's $.60 charge for long-distance information.

Shop Talk

Over the phone or face-to-face with a front-desk clerk, inexperienced hagglers should *negotiate with euphemisms*. Instead of declaring an all-out bidding war, ask the clerk whether the hotel has a "corporate rate" or "commercial rate," a deal for business travelers that hotels often grant anyone who asks for it. Inquire whether discounts exist for members of any constituency to which you belong—senior citizens, students, teachers, union members, auto-club members, airline frequent-flyer club participants, astigmatic Norwegian seamstresses, and the like. Even if one never existed before, desire for your patronage could occasion an extemporaneous discount program. Or tell them you own stock in the company. Some hotel chains (Marriott, for example) have special stockholders' rates. These rates may apply only when the hotel occupancy is below a certain level.

If the hotel doesn't bite on any of these ploys, you probably won't get far. But if you get a cut-rate offer that falls short of your specifications, don't hesitate to make a *counteroffer*. "That much? I was hoping to find something around. . . . " Now the hotel clerk knows what you want and, since he or she suspects that you'll go next door or down the street to get it, you'll force his (her) hand.

Be circumspect and ask if the hotel has any cheaper *rooms without bath*, free or discounted rates for *extra nights*, or *weekly rates*. Offer to pay *cash*, an option that saves the hotel the charge-card commission and may give the hotelier certain sub-rosa tax advantages. Or boldly set a limit and challenge the hotel to meet it: "I will spend no more than $25 for a room. Do you have anything at that price?"

Without Reservations

If you have no reason to believe the area might possess more hotel rooms than guests who want them, begin shopping where several hotels are located. Having choices provides a crucial psychological advantage in bargaining for hotels (or anything else, for that matter). If you don't get what you want, you can easily take your business elsewhere. You know this, and the hotel knows you know it.

Set a price before you initiate negotiations. Decide on an opening offering and the price above which you absolutely, positively will not pay. Be realistic, but don't hesitate to set your sights low. You can always raise your limit, but it's comforting to know that you started with an offer they *could* refuse.

Don't expect to haggle too successfully until *later in the day*, when hotels have a better idea of how many rooms are likely to be vacant. In fact, don't begin until after 6:00 P.M., the usual time rooms that have been reserved but not guaranteed with a charge card (charging guests for the room even if they never show up) become available. Of course, the later you arrive, the more desperate the hotel will be to rent a room at any price.

The thing to remember is that under certain market conditions it is you, not the hotel, who holds the upper hand. At the time in the evening when the hotel knows it will not be fully occupied, it needs you more than you need it. If it can, a hotel will always try to get you to pay the "rack rate," the hotel-industry equivalent of an appliance dealer's "list price" and the airlines' "normal coach fare"; if it can't, it might be amenable to your best offer.

"Nearly everybody rates a hotel discount: When making reservations or checking in, inquire whether your employment situation, professional or fraternal affiliation, age, motor club or frequent-flyer program membership, or anything else qualifies for a cut rate."

———————◈ TRAVELER'S ALERT ◈———————

Don't be intimidated by clerks in hotels with empty rooms. Don't hesitate to ask for a shamelessly low rate. Don't be afraid to walk if you can't get the deal you want. And don't be too proud to return to a hotel where the deal you spurned turns out to be the best you can get.

BED & BREAKFASTS

The Bed & Breakfast concept comes from the British Isles, where institutions catering to budget-minded pleasure and business travelers are found in every village and town. A significant component of the British lodging industry, a B & B might be anything from a small hotel to rooms in a private home. Comfort levels range from Spartan to homey to deluxe. The only thing you can count on is the traditionally hearty British breakfast of juice, eggs, bacon, sausage, toast and marmalade, and coffee or tea.

The B & B idea, whose time has just come to the United States, is quite a different animal. Although American B & Bs generally cost less than the best hotels or resorts, they principally appeal as cozy alternatives to the impersonal, contemporary business hotel. B & Bs have a small number of rooms, each usually as different as the guests who inhabit them. Instead of the "no surprises" ambience offered by the large international hotel chains, B & Bs are owned and operated by families or couples whose physical presence and quirky tastes are readily apparent.

U.S.A.-Style B & Bs

The B & Bs in the United States come in several distinctive flavors. *Pure B & Bs* are honest-to-goodness family homes where guests eat, socialize, and perhaps share bathrooms with family members.

The most common form of B & B are *B & B inns*, usually large old houses that have been converted into small hotels. Although guests have ample opportunity to mingle with their hosts and fellow guests, they usually eat at separate tables and often have private baths.

The third style is the *B & B hotel*, a somewhat spurious designation for a small hotel trying to get into the B & B act by adding a free-breakfast program.

Price is not the main advantage of B & Bs. Though cheaper than first-class lodgings in a particular locality, B & Bs usually cost more than budget motels. Because rates are entirely contingent upon location, quality of accommodations, and proprietor caprice, prices range from $10 a room to well into three figures.

B & B Pros and Cons

The main advantages of B & Bs are the quality of the accommodations, the individualized charm of the rooms, the homelike atmosphere, the personal attention of the hosts, and sometimes the food. Since these establishments are usually located in "real" neighborhoods rather than in commercial districts or resort ghettos, they afford closer contact with the life of a particular area. Many B & Bs encourage neighborliness among guests by hosting afternoon teas or wine-and-cheese hours.

B & Bs can be found everywhere now—in resort areas, small towns, and the largest metropolises. Many people, particularly escapees from the big city, fancy B & Bs because they are reminiscent of the homes in which they used to live or wish they could return to.

Two main styles of hosts operate B & B establishments today: local people who have turned the old family home into an income-producing property and outsiders, generally refugees from urban environs, for whom owning and operating a B & B represents a fantasy fulfilled. Both categories of hosts tend to be hardworking "people persons" who enjoy talking about their community, local happenings, antique hunting, and the joys of operating a B & B.

The disadvantages of B & Bs are inherent aspects of their appeal. They are not full-service hotels and thus lack amenities you would expect from even the meanest of lodging places—namely in-room phones, TVs, pools, snack shops, and ice machines.

Finding B & Bs requires some initiative on your part, and making a reservation can be something of a hassle. B & Bs don't have toll-free reservation numbers, and sometimes nobody's home to answer the phone. Most B & Bs require advance deposits to hold a reservation, and many do not accept charge cards.

Many travelers have problems with the personalized touch that is a B & B's bread and butter. You may not hit it off with your host, the family, or the other guests. If you don't relish the unexpected and prefer not to mingle, the B & B bill of fare may not be your cup of tea.

Sometimes B & B accommodations themselves are not up to snuff. The most common complaints are rooms that are too small, too noisy, or too close to screaming children. Sometimes guests are allergic to the host's pets. A frequent complaint is that B & B guidebooks exaggerate the virtues of their listings. *Seventeen* editor Kathy Rich characterized one listed New York City B & B she once stayed in as "the moral equivalent of crashing on the couch" and claimed that she had to pass through the bedroom of a "woman of easy virtue" to reach the bathroom.

Finding B & Bs

To separate what's quaint from what ain't, there is no substitute for the hearty personal recommendation of someone well-experienced in matters B & B. Barring that, there are three principal methods of finding these establishments.

One is the old reliable *Yellow Pages*, which since 1982 has included a special heading for "Bed & Breakfast Accommodations." Check out listings in out-of-town phone books in the public library or look them up as soon as you hit town.

B & Bs are, for the most part, small establishments which may devote their entire marketing budget to classified ads in a nearby *big city daily newspaper*. Ads run in Sunday travel sections or in daily editions under the heading of "Vacations" or "Hotels." Some papers carry a profusion of B & B ads. Under the heading "Small Inns & Lodges," the Sunday *New York Times* travel section runs up to three pages of classified listings for establishments along the Eastern Seaboard from Maine to the Carolinas. Similarly, the travel section in the Sunday *San Francisco Examiner & Chronicle* lists northern California resorts under "Small Inns & Resorts."

City, state, and regional magazines invariably carry classifieds for B & Bs in the vicinity.

Suddenly recognizing the visitor appeal of B & Bs, many *state, city, and regional tourism offices* publicize B & Bs and Reservation Service Organizations (see below) in their free promotional literature. Some farsighted dominions—among them Massachusetts, North Carolina, and Minnesota—publish special guides to B & Bs. For toll-free phone numbers of state tourism offices, see "Appendix."

B & B Guidebooks

Another major source of information are the numerous *guidebooks* published in recent years. Usually available in annually updated regional editions, guidebooks generally include detailed descriptions of the establishments themselves, thumbnail personality sketches of the hosts, a rating of the cuisine, and something about the area. Here are some of the best:

Affordable B & Bs: $40 or Less for Two People, by Loris G. Bree (MarLor Press, St. Paul, $9.95). The only thing wrong with this commendable book is that it's far too short.

Bed & Breakfast America: The Great American Guest House Book, by John Thaxton (Burt Franklin, New York, $8.95). This chatty and attractive guide lists B & Bs and RSOs nationwide.

Bed & Breakfast Coast to Coast, by Bernice Chesler (Stephen Greene Press, Lexington [MA], $12.95). Over 200 RSOs with access to 15,000 accommodations in the U.S. and Canada are included.

The Bed & Breakfast Guide for the U.S. Canada, Bermuda, Puerto Rico, and U.S. Virgin Islands, by Phyllis Featherston and Barbara F. Ostler (National Bed & Breakfast Association, Norwalk [CT]. $11.95). A listing of the over 1,000 members of the National Bed & Breakfast Association, this guide features concise charts and capsule descriptions supplied by proprietors.

Bed & Breakfast U.S.A., Betty Rundback and Nancy Ackerman (Dutton, $9.95). This book provides a concise listing of more than 800 nationwide "tourist homes and guest houses" and more than 150 reservation services as well as information on starting your own.

Bed & Breakfast American Style, Norman T. Simpson (Berkshire Traveller Press, $10.95). Featured in this publication are more than 420 detailed (full-page) descriptions of B & Bs in thirty-two states, Canada, and New Zealand.

The Complete Guide to B & B's, Inns & Guesthouses, Pamela Lanier (John Muir Publications, $12.95). A total of 2,800 inns, 10,000 private guest homes, and 300 reservation services are listed in this publication.

Fodor's Bed & Breakfast Guide, by Mary Winget (Fodor's Travel Publications, New York, $9.95). Uniquely (but not too helpfully), Fodor's contains neither names, addresses, nor phone numbers for the B & Bs it lists. Instead, it provides capsule descriptions, amenity codes, and a "Reservation Contact" for each establishment.

Frommer's Bed & Breakfast North America, by Hal Gieseking (Prentice Hall, New York, $8.95) *Frommer's* provides up-to-date information on 150 RSOs and 200 inns.

Guide to the Recommended Country Inns Series, by various authors (Globe Pequot Press, Chester [CT], $9.95) This series contains extremely thorough, subjective, and entertaining descriptions of country inns, lodges, B & Bs, etc. Separate editions are available on the Midwest, New England, Mid-Atlantic/Chesapeake Region, West Coast, South, Rocky Mountain Region, Texas and the Southwest.

Sleep Cheap: A Directory of Tourist Homes and B & Bs in the United States & Canada, by Jon & Nancy Kugelman (McBride/Publisher, Hartford, $6.95). *Sleep Cheap* lists 1,400 establishments in 49 states and 10 Canadian provinces. Available by mail from: McBride/Publisher, 157 Sisson Ave., Hartford, CT 06105 (add $1 postage).

Books listed here are available in general-interest bookstores and bookstores specializing in travel: See appendix for "Booksellers."

Reservation-Service Organizations

The other way to book a B & B is to contact a *reservation-service organization* (RSO). RSOs tend to be as idiosyncratic as the B & Bs they represent. Some operate nationwide and serve hundreds of B & Bs around the country; others list only a handful of places in a specific community.

Some RSOs function merely as reservation services, recommending guests only according to where and when they need accommodations. Others regard themselves as matchmakers who need to discover enough about the callers' personality, tastes, and circumstances to fix them up with the ideal host.

There are more than 300 RSOs operating nationwide, and they can be located through local tourist-information offices. Here are some of the major regional, national, international, and specialized B & B RSOs:

American Bed & Breakfast Association (P.O. Box 23294, Washington, DC 20026; 703-237-9777). This is a B & B umbrella organization that publishes directories of individual B & Bs, a directory to local RSOs, and a host kit explaining how you can become a B & B host.

Bed & Breakfast Reservation Services Worldwide, Inc., (P.O. Box 14797, Dept. 174, Baton Rouge, LA 70898; 504-346-1928). To receive a listing of 75 RSOs in the U.S., Canada, England, France, and New Zealand, send $1 and a business-sized self-addressed stamped envelope. Then contact RSOs themselves for directories which range in price from free to $5. A B&BRSWW newsletter, *Around the World with Bed & Breakfast,* contains general information and descriptions of particular B & Bs. For a one-year subscription (six issues) and RSO directory, send $20 to above address. Make check payable to "B&BRSWW-Newsletter."

Bed & Breakfast: The National Network (P.O. Box 4616, Springfield, MA 01101; 413-783-5764). This is an association of twenty-three local reservation services located from coast to coast.

Bed & Breakfast Registry (P. O. Box 8174, St. Paul, MN 55108; 612-646-4238). A reservation service for more than 300 B & Bs in thirty-five states as well as Washington, D.C. and Puerto Rico, this organization has a preponderance of listings for the Northeast, California, and Minnesota.

Educator's Inn (P.O. Box 603, Lynnfield, MA 01940). A network of B & Bs in thirty-four states and five foreign countries, this organization exists exclusively for educators and the educational-system support staff. A lifetime membership fee of $9.95 and proof of educational employment are required.

Sweet Dreams & Toast (P.O. Box 4835-0035, Washington, DC 20008; 202-483-9191). A B & B reservation service for the Washington, D.C., area, Sweet Dreams & Toast distributes *Bed & Breakfast Services—United States,* a listing of more than 200 local RSOs in forty-three states and Washington, D.C. To receive this extremely valuable, concise pamphlet, send $3 to the above address.

Urban Ventures (P.O. Box 426, New York, NY 10024; 212-594-5650). More than 800 B & Bs and unoccupied apartments in Manhattan and New York City area are listed by this organization.

HOME EXCHANGES

A home exchange is one way to "live like the Romans" for next to no *lire*. By swapping your home for that of a like-minded stranger, you save on hotel bills, get space and facilities for cooking and entertaining, and stay in a real neighborhood rather than in a tourist ghetto. A great way to travel with children, the home exchange may extend to the use of cars, boats, country-club privileges, and even household help and baby-sitters.

Of course, to get a piece of this action you must have a home to exchange. And you must be willing to allow strangers to have the same run of your house that you expect to have in theirs. You also have to make the arrangements and negotiate the terms yourself.

Unfortunately, many of us are probably disqualified before we start. With respect to arranging a trade, the condition of your residence is less critical than its location. Let's face it, if you have a cottage on Cape Cod, a chalet in Aspen, or a townhouse in San Francisco, home swappers worldwide will beat a path to your door. But if you live in a geographically undesirable clime (I won't imperil sales by naming names; you know who you are), your chances are next to nil.

Trading Places

If your home is physically and geographically fit, you can advertise for a trade. One approach is to place an ad in the classified section of the newspaper or city magazine of your prospective destination. You can obtain addresses and ad rates for U.S. and international publications by checking the annual *Ulrich's Guides*, which are available in most public libraries.

If you are flexible about destination and would prefer to swap with someone with whom you have something in common, advertise in a special-interest publication. Advertisements placed in publications devoted to those who share hobbies, artistic pursuits, or political slants will presumably attract those who speak the same cultural language. This doesn't mean that if you're a left-wing chess fanatic from Portland, a left-wing chess fanatic from Barcelona won't run up the phone bill or burn a hole in the rug. But the more comfortable you feel about the people staying in your home, the more comfortable you'll feel in theirs.

In any case, when writing the ad, describe your home as if it were for sale. Describe the kind of home you're looking for and the approximate dates of availability, and make dates of availability as flexible as possible.

Home-Exchange Clubs

Most of the home exchanges that do take place—and there are thousands every year—are facilitated by directories published by *home-exchange clubs*. The advantage of using these clubs is that your listing is seen by a multitude of potential swappers who otherwise may not have considered your location. Similarly, you are exposed to numerous locational options. Directory listings are reasonably priced and usually cost much less than ads in national magazines or major daily newspapers. In general, exchange clubs are a very economical way of reaching the precise audience you seek.

Home-exchange clubs operate as passive matchmakers. They do not inspect the houses to guarantee the accuracy of the listings; nor do they participate in the exchange process itself. Rather, they function like the personals ads, printing whatever advertisers send and permitting principals to make their own arrangements.

The *Vacation Exchange Club* (12006 111th Avenue, Youngtown, AZ 85363; 602-972-2186) is the oldest (founded in 1960) and largest home-exchange club in the United States. Half of the 6,000 listings in its most recent directory were for homes in 40 foreign countries, principally Great Britain, Germany, Italy, Spain, Portugal, and Scandinavia. Listings in the United States usually consist of first or second homes located along the Atlantic and Pacific coasts. The area with the biggest unmet demand is New England, where home owners generally find it easier (and more profitable) to rent outright than to swap.

If you contact the Vacation Exchange Club you will receive a subscription form asking for detailed information about your home and family. In the "location" section, you write your state or residence and whether the setting is urban, suburban, rural, shore, or mountains; also include the nearest major city and the distance from that city. The "period" section asks when your home is available and whether dates are flexible or firm. The "transactions" section requires you to stipulate which of various deals options you would like to make: exchange, rental, or double exchange involving two families in each area, among others.

The personal information section asks for your name, address, and phone number; your occupation; the number of adults involved, teenagers, and children traveling in your group; and foreign countries or areas of the United States you would like to visit. To describe your home, you encode whether it is a one-story house, a multiple-story house, an apartment, vacation home, or mobile home; the number of bedrooms, bathrooms; and the number of persons it can comfortably accommodate.

A final section permits you to encode information about particular features of your home (air conditioning, barbecue, garden, garage, elevator, among others); local activities (golf, skiing, tennis, and the like); area attractions (beach, museums, theaters); extras (baby-sitter, use of boat, car, bicycles); caveats (car necessary; no children, pets, smokers); miscellaneous information; and language preferred for correspondence. This section also has space for "free words," which enables you to include information that it is not possible to encode, for instance, "wine cellar," "two hrs from Yosemite," "fine view of mountains."

Vacation Exchange publishes a directory twice a year—the main directory in February and a supplement in April. The deadline for the February issue is December 15; for the April issue, February 15. Subscribers pay $24.70 for a listing in either of the books and receive copies of both. Listings for each additional home cost $6.00 apiece, and running a photo (optional) costs $9.00. Unlisted subscribers interested in straight rentals can pay $16 for copies of both books.

Vacation Exchange Club says that the more flexible you can be as to date and time, the more likely you are to find a good exchange. For this reason people who have to be someplace on a particular date are not encouraged to go this route. They also advise you to leave sufficient time for corresponding about potential trades—at least a couple of months and perhaps more for overseas exchanges.

Although the Vacation Exchange Club does not inspect the homes listed in its directory or guarantee the accuracy of these listings, it claims that its properties are generally nicely maintained middle-class homes and that many are even quite luxurious. They advise swappers to spell out all financial arrangements in detail, particularly with respect to phone charges, car usage, and damage deposits. Vacation Exchange cautions that "swappers" tend to take better care of homes than "renters," but they have never had any serious problems involving damage or theft.

Other Home-Exchange Clubs

Home Exchange International (185 Park Row, P.O. Box 878, New York, NY 10038-0272; 212-349-5340). This agency uses detailed descriptions and photos provided by the owners to match applicants seeking exchanges. They have representatives in London, Milan, and Paris; most sought-after areas include Florida, Manhattan, and France. Applicants pay one-time $40 registration fee and closing fee of $150–$525 depending on location and duration of exchange.

Worldwide Exchange (P.O. Box 1563, San Leandro, CA 94577; 415-521-7890). Subscribers pay $19.95 for a listing in any of four annual directories. Listings also appear on the CompuServe data base.

Intervac (P.O. Box 3975, San Francisco, CA 94119; 415-435-3497). Approximately 4,000 homes in twenty countries are listed three times a year (January, March, May) by Intervac. Listings and copies of all three books cost $35; unlisted subscriptions are $45.

Loan-A-Home (2 Park Lane-6E, Mount Vernon, NY 10552; 914-664-7640). This organization is geared to "members of the international academic and business community and their families who need temporary housing" in cities, resort areas, and academic centers throughout the world. It publishes a directory four times a year—December, March, June, and September. There is no charge for listing; two directories cost $20, four $30.

THE ART OF "GUESTING"

Theoretically, staying at the home of a friend or relative is the cheapest form of lodging. Theoretically, it is free. But what guests save on rent they may pay in psychic coin that easily nudges the practice into the more-trouble-than-it's-worth class. "Guesting" is a social art; here are guidelines for producing masterpieces both guest and host can savor.

Guest-Friendly Households

Each household style has advantages and drawbacks. Visitors to *singles* households may attract the undivided attention of the host, a situation that can be burdensome.

Couples can be pleasant hosts since the hosts will probably be happy to have someone come in and break up the routine. But unless you feel like spending your vacation serving as a couples counselor or referee, avoid couples households where internal tension is known to exist.

You can get lost in the shuffle of complicated *families* consisting of parents that juggle jobs and children and pets. These situations are great for eye-of-the-hurricane privacy but not so great for personal attention.

Guest Guidelines

1. *Never arrive unexpectedly.* Allow your host as much time as possible to prepare for your arrival. This benefits both of you: The host can arrange a schedule if he or she is wont to entertain, and this also allows time to stock up on your favorite goodies.

2. *Inform your host of exactly how long you intend to stay.* This is important. You can always alter your plans, but a firm "reservation" alleviates pressure on everybody. How long should you stay? This depends entirely on the destination, your relationship with the host, the household style, and how much your presence disrupts it. As a rule of thumb, however, stay no longer than three days in a house or apartment in which you have no private bedroom and no longer than a week anywhere.

3. *Arrive bearing gifts.* Barring anything traditional or sentimentally evocative, bring things that can be collected rather than exhibited. Books, records, videotapes—good; pictures, ashtrays, anything that might have to be dragged out of the storage the next time you come—less good. Liquor or fine wine is always welcome; food seldom is. Either somebody is on some diet or somebody thinks somebody should be. Food is controversial. Good guests shouldn't risk taking sides, even inadvertently. These principles also apply to the *de rigueur* thank-you gift.

4. *Pitch in on all the usual chores—washing dishes, yardwork—and plus be creative.* Every household at which I have ever guested has one particular chore that for reason unfathomable to outsiders has become an issue and an ordeal. For the astute houseguest, this "Achilles' chore" represents a golden opportunity. Take it off your hosts' hands and, regardless of how thin your welcome otherwise wears, they will never ask you to leave. It is easy to discover the nature of this chore; listen closely and you will hear a direct or oblique reference to it within fifteen minutes of arrival.

The odd thing is that the chore is usually more repetitive and intrusive than inherently loathsome. In one household I visited, it meant walking the dog twice a day. Taking out garbage, mowing lawns, or shoveling snow are common hassles. The "Achilles' chore" can also be a one-shot unknotting of a touchy family problem. Friends in Chicago named me Guest of the Year merely for acquiring (for $3.98) a gas cap for their foreign car.

5. *Don't assume that meals are provided; arrange to be elsewhere when mealtime comes around.* Since the demise of the fulltime housewife, most households have serious problems with food—what to eat, who prepares it, who shops, among other things. If the host specifically invites you for a meal, you must accept; otherwise fend for yourself.

6. *The bathroom is a sensitive area.* You would probably prefer not to have too much specific information about your host's bathroom routines, but the unobtrusive houseguest must know them by rote. You can't go wrong if you take your morning shower *before* everybody else. Failing that opportunity, wait until they're all done. What if they don't take showers? Should you ask? As I said, houseguesting can accrue potentially exorbitant psychic costs.

7. *Don't sleep late*, at least no later than the latest sleeping household member. People tend to morally censure those who sleep later than themselves, and no host likes to tiptoe around his own home. Also, make your bed the moment you rise. Keep clothes out of the way. Don't smoke if your host disapproves.

8. *Don't charge long-distance calls to the host's phone.* Even if it makes sense to you to ask the operator for charges and pay on the spot, don't do it. When the bill comes a month later, it will irritate the host to shell out the money for your call *even if he or she does remember that you paid.* This is yet another irrational human foible to which a guest may fall victim. You can avoid retrospective annoyance by charging the call to your home phone, using an AT&T calling card, or signing up for an alternative long-distance service like Sprint, which permits low-priced away-from-home calls.

Guest Rights

On the other hand, guests have rights too, and it's a mistake to spoil a vacation by being too meek to demand them.

1. *A place to sleep*—not necessarily a private room but somewhere to lay your head.

2. *Basic linens*—towels, washcloth, sheets, pillow cases, blankets—and it is not "pushy" to ask for them.

3. *Breakfast.* It doesn't have to be lavish—juice, coffee, a roll are acceptable—but a guest is entitled to some nourishment before leaving the home.

4. *A key.* If the host doesn't have a spare, offer to have one made at your expense—but get that key. This one precaution eliminates hassles that pertain to coordinating schedules, coming in late, returning in the afternoon, and innumerable other tension areas.

Further concessions are subject to the thoughtfulness and generosity of the host.

Visiting Hours

How you spend your visit largely depends upon the disposition of your host. Some hosts consider the free bed a sufficient gesture of friendship and deem entertainment services above and beyond the call of duty. This is more likely to be the case in high-volume guest cities like New York, San Francisco, and Paris, and at resort paradises like Aspen, Taos, and Honolulu. In these locations, the gracious guest would do well to become informed about a particular destination and make individual plans.

Some hosts, however, expect to entertain you (or vice versa). They concoct detailed itineraries and consider independent plans a breach of friendship. If you're not sure where your host is coming from, make plans on your own and invite the host to come along. In either case, be sure to invite your host for at least one splurge meal or night on the town. Suggest someplace they've always wanted to go but for some reason never have. Make it clear from the start that you are paying for everything.

Guesting falls into the high savings/high stress range of lodging alternatives. You can save up to 100 percent of your lodging costs, but you can also be 100 percent miserable if you waste your vacation in physical and psychological discomfort. If the hosts have guest facilities and you have the guest mentality, go for it. Otherwise, in the interest of preserving the relationship, stay at a nearby motel.

THE SCIENCE OF HOSTING

The science of hosting complements the art of guesting. Guest around enough, and you must eventually reciprocate. Obviously the areas of concern discussed in the previous section are identical for host and guest. Tragically, you cannot assume that your guests have read that section, so the burden of the guest/host interaction may fall upon you. It is vital for a host to set things straight at the start.

1. Find out exactly how long guests intend to stay; if it sounds too long say so before they arrive.

2. Inform guests about house hours—whether you get up early and make noise, and if it would be terribly inconvenient if they strolled in during the middle of the night.

3. Go over the drill for meals, ideally allowing guests to prepare breakfast for themselves.

4. Outline your schedule for the course of the visit, pointing out to your guests when it is convenient for you to spend time with them. If you would prefer one particular time for your thanks-for-the-hospitality dinner, pass this on to your guests.

5. State ground rules for smoking, alcohol, kitchen privileges, and the guest's guest privileges.

6. Show guests how everything works—TV, stereo, door locks, eccentric plumbing. Tell guests when they should not play the stereo, watch TV, or otherwise manufacture noise.

7. Explain any idiosyncratic house rules you expect your guests to observe. (I live in Manhattan; guests are forbidden under threat of expulsion to repeat panhandlers' spiels or describe *anything* they see on the subway.)

8. Encourage guest self-sufficiency. As a nondirective type of host, I have assembled a survival kit containing street map, subway map, and bus map, address locator, Michelin guide to New York City, a calendar of quarterly events, and an invaluable little book entitled *Dear John* (by Lana Toni Gersman, Tribeca Communications, $2.95), a directory/critique of Manhattan washrooms. On bestowing kit and key, I declare guests officially on their own.

Depending on the degree of guest welcomeness and host graciousness, you may want to spend more time and take more care. Ideally, the guest/host relationship should obey a *Cheap/Smart Travel* Golden Rule: Do unto guest as you would have guest, as host, do unto you.

SIX

FOOD

RESTAURANT RECOMMENDATIONS

Tips in this section are not intended to save money on food at the expense of all other considerations. Whereas rock-bottom prices may be a laudable goal with respect to transportation and lodging, eating dirt-cheap may defeat the very purpose of travel. The goal, then, is to guide you toward the best values on the most distinctive food a locality has to offer.

A Feast of Disclaimers

There are *no rules* for finding good restaurants, no rules of thumb, and not even a rule of a pinky finger. I can't generalize that all hotel restaurants are expensive and terrible (though many are) any more than I can claim that they are at least adequate. No formulas—"the restaurant next door to a police station"; "places bearing Italian women's names"—work. Such universal verities as exist are limited to facetious dicta—"Never eat in places called Ma's . . . " (Nelson Algren)—or demonstrably bad advice—"Try roadside restaurants where you see a lot of trucks because truckers know good food." (Anon.)

The subject of restaurant quality is also too much a matter of personal opinion to attack with consumeristic zeal. Between a few great restaurants everybody loves and others too poor to stomach lies a chasm of subjectivity in which everything is reduced to a matter of taste.

In the absence of rules and a proliferation of subjectivity, my best advice involves methods for locating sources of informed and impartial information wherever you go.

Who *Not* to Ask

There are people whom you should never ask for restaurant recommendations. This category begins with those who are asked frequently and may therefore be in a position to profit by their recommendations. Unless you know them or have reason to trust them, *don't ask a concierge, desk clerk, bellman, porter, doorman, or anyone else who works in a hotel*. Too often they will be more loyal to a relative or friend in the restaurant business than to you. Hotel employees are frequently reimbursed for sending guests to certain restaurants. Be especially wary if a hotel employee scribbles his name on a restaurant's business card and tells you to present it for red-carpet treatment.

Don't even think about asking *cab drivers* for a restaurant recommendation. Cab drivers are not known for discriminating palates, and many restaurants reward them for delivering customers to the door. Even if they don't have sweetheart arrangements with restaurants, the economics of the taxi business rewards drivers for recommending as the best restaurant the one farthest from wherever they find you.

Who *to* Ask

Rather than relying on "professional" recommenders, try your luck with disinterested locals. *Store clerks* are excellent sources. They are obliged to talk to you and should know about restaurants near their shop. *People in the retail food business*—grocers, butchers, bakers, fishmongers—tend to be especially knowledgeable and discriminating sources of information on good places in the neighborhood.

Try passengers who sit beside you on the bus or people who are beside you in line. Most people take a kind of chauvinistic pride in their favorite eateries and are happy to steer strangers in that direction.

The best guide to good local restaurants nationwide is *Road Food & Good Food* by Jane and Michael Stern (Knopf, $10.95). Divided into regions and sub-divided by state, the book includes restaurants where you can best enjoy all the local color while partaking of deliciously indigenous dining experiences. The six-volume *Interstate Gourmet* series (Summit Books, $6.95 apiece) lists tasty, reasonably-priced alternatives to franchise fare located at nearly every highway interchange and within most towns.

How to Ask

One secret is to *categorize* your request. If you ask for the best restaurant in town, nine times out of ten they send you to the Hilton or some other overpriced joint with a better press agent than a chef. Instead, ask for a good place to get a steak, seafood, Mexican food, or health food. If you are aware of any regional specialty—for instance, barbecue (a noun, not an adjective) in North Carolina, crab cakes in Baltimore, or chili in Texas—ask your sources where *they* go for these treats. Indicate that price *is* an object and ask how much it is likely to cost. People brag on the cheapness of their pet places as much as on their ambience, friendliness, and cuisine.

Another secret is to *keep asking until you reach a consensus*. If three of the five San Franciscans recommend the same sushi bar, that's probably the one you want. In all cases, ascertain whether the recommender has *personal experience* at the place, preferably a recent one. Like hearsay evidence, hearsay recommendations are totally inadmissible.

Fellow Travelers

The problem with even the most well-intentioned locals is that the request for a restaurant recommendation often activates a latent strain of civic boosterism. They may deem the place they habituate as insufficiently grand or sophisticated and instead send you someplace they heard was supposed to be great. You, however, are not writing a brief for their city; you are interested in eating good, inexpensive indigenous food.

Consequently, the best source of recommendation may not be locals but *experienced travelers* who know the dining places that best express the city's peculiar charm. Finding these experienced travelers may be a challenge. If you know of people who visit a city frequently, ask them for recommendations. A seatmate on a plane or airport limo into town may be a good source. Barring that, you could try a bar at one of the major hotels, always an active swapmart of restaurant tips.

How to Read City Magazines

Anyplace that's anyplace boasts a monthly or weekly city magazine, and every city magazine has a comprehensive and timely restaurant guide. Directed more to locals than visitors, city-magazine listings include bread-and-butter information on type of cuisine, hours, credit-card acceptance, reservation requirements, and proper attire.

The city guide's appraisal of quality, however, is subject to closer scrutiny. Some city-guide listings consist of capsule reviews assembled by objective staff members; others merely include advertisers and make no pretense of objectivity.

Fortunately, most city magazines freely reveal their true colors. The preface to the dining section of *Chicago Guide* states: "These listings are limited to recommended dinner restaurants that have been rated exceptional for food quality and/or variety, service, ambience, and value, after visits by our staff reviewers. There is no relation to advertising." Similarly, *Houston City Magazine* says: "Our listings are revised and supplemented periodically. Visits by our critics are made anonymously to avoid preferential treatment. *Inclusion in this directory has nothing whatever to do with paid advertising.*"

On the other hand, the restaurant directory in *New York Magazine* states: "This is a list of advertisers plus some of the city's most popular dining establishments." And *Boston Magazine* admits: "All information in the listings is supplied to *Boston Magazine* by the restaurants, and we cannot guarantee its accuracy. . . . Because of space limitations, only restaurants that advertise in *Boston Magazine* are included in the guide." Oh. It seems that when consulting the restaurant guide of a city magazine, it pays to read the fine print.

FORAGING FOR RESTAURANTS

Chronic shyness, acute language barrier, or sheer cussed determination to do it "your way" may impel you to try to sniff out good, cheap restaurants on your own. This is the essence of adventure travel and an occasion where a flamboyant failure may be more memorable than a safe success. There are, however, a few things you can do to tilt the odds in your favor.

Places to Avoid

First, avoid restaurants in *areas frequented by people who do not pay checks with their own money*, i.e., business travelers. This embargo pertains for the most part to restaurants in and around major hotels. The food may or may not be good, but in either case it will bear a substantial surcharge for convenience that is not imposed elsewhere in the city.

"To find a good, cheap, interesting restaurant in a strange town, head for an ethnic neighborhood or university campus."

For similar reasons, avoid the *central business district* of any large city. Any area nicknamed "the Wall Street of Wherever" is the land of the long expense account and lunchtime stampede—and no place at all to find a bargain.

Don't expect to find good, cheap restaurants in *remote or isolated locations*. This emphatically applies to airports, bus stations, and to the notoriously mediocre concessions in tourist attractions. You want a rule of thumb? O.K., you got a rule of thumb: Whenever possible, eat where the sole economic activity is food preparation and service. This rule eliminates eating places in hotels, airports, bus stations, ball parks, and theme parks. It encompasses only those enterprises that live or die by the quality of their food.

Where to Eat

Where are you most likely to track down a good place to eat? Every city has ethnic groups, every ethnic group a neighborhood, and every ethnic neighborhood a multitude of restaurants. Since restaurants in any "Ethnictown" must vie for the custom of knowledgeable and discriminating area residents, they tend to be excellent and relatively inexpensive. Get yourself to Chinatown in New York or San Francisco, the Greek neighborhoods of Detroit and Chicago (there are two), the Spanish/Cuban Ybor City section of Tampa, and you virtually cannot go wrong.

Commercial areas contiguous to any *university* are always extremely promising. Since students tend to have adventurous tastes and shallow pockets, collegetowns invariably boast scads of low-price restaurants serving all the latest recherche cuisines. These days you can count on collegetowns for exotic self-service (which means no tip) fast-food establishments—falafel, gyros, empañadas, croissant sandwiches, and whatever other trends come down the pike.

If your destination lacks an outright collegetown, it may still have what I hesitantly call a "young hip section." Strangers in town can find it by employing the *Casablanca Method*. Turn to the movie section of the local paper; find the local "revival house"— if *Casablanca* doesn't happen to be playing that day, it will be showing a foreign-language film or another Hollywood classic; proceed hence. Within a two-block area surrounding the revival house, you will invariably find an assortment of reasonably priced restaurants from around the Orient, a decent fish place, a health-food restaurant, several coffee houses, and a fairly cheap French-style bistro. (In cities where the Casablanca method cannot be used, the Comedy Store Method has proved effective.)

—————————— ◈ TRAVELER'S ALERT ◈ ——————————

Read the menus posted outside to get some idea of how much you are likely to spend; avoid restaurants that don't post menus. Even in New York City, the rip-off restaurant capital of America, almost every restaurant displays a menu.

Many restaurants post clippings of newspaper and restaurant reviews in conspicuous exterior locations. Read them: The mere existence of the review does not ensure a positive appraisal. Beware of places that display reviews more than two years old. If they haven't been praised lately, chances are they declined after the old review made them hot.

FAST FOOD JOINTS: AN APPRECIATION

I used to be a fast-food snob. I boycotted fast-food chains and heaped scorn upon their patrons. I did this not because of the blandness of the food or its dubious nutritional value or moral qualms following from the unsupported presumption that to create the traffic necessary to support each McDonald's or Taco Bell, about seventeen homey folksy Mom-and-Pop diners had to bite the dust.

These were secondary considerations. My real objection was that fast-food places were *unadventurous*. Eating fast food sacrificed a potentially unforgettable indigenous eating experience in favor of a humdrum sure thing. Eating fast food wasn't exactly bad, but it was cowardly, lazy, much too easy.

Primary and secondary objections aside, I have lately felt more compassion for the plight of other travelers and myself. Travel, I now see, is among the most demanding of human endeavors. Travelers must incessantly satisfy creature needs in unfamiliar surroundings, possibly accommodate the needs of others in the same circumstances, constantly spend more money than anticipated, and have splendid fun every single second because that's the point of it all. An obsession with doing everything on the cheap may make this maelstrom of perpetual decision making more than the human psyche can bear.

A Therapeutic Respite

I now concede that a respite of predictable mediocrity—particularly when it costs less than a stressful adventure—can be therapeutic. That's where fast-food joints come in.

Fast-food restaurants are modern-day incarnations of Hemingway's "clean, well-lighted place." Indeed, they are literally clean and extremely well lighted—franchise agreements are usually quite explicit on these points. But they also fulfill Hemingway's symbolic specifications: Safe and welcoming, open early, late, sometimes never closing at all, fast-food restaurants are there when you need them.

You can relax in a fast-food restaurant. No hovering waitperson shames you for hogging a table or not spending enough money. You can relax over a paper cup of nondairy "shake" and peruse road map, guidebook, or newspaper to your heart's content. It seems to be no one's job to make you leave when you finish your meal.

Yes, the food is predictable, bland, unindigenous—unadventurous. But how many of us can handle culinary adventures three or four times a day? And, arguably, the adventure-seeking capacity you don't expend on choosing a quaint place for lunch can be profitably recycled later in the search for a perfect dinner.

Another very big plus for fast-food joints is their rest rooms. Since the gas-station rest room fell into disrepute, fast-food places have become the best bathrooms on the road. They're better than gas stations, actually, because you don't have to ask anybody for the key. Even if you're not hungry, you can stop to use the clean, well-lighted john.

MALLS: A MULTIPURPOSE SANCTUARY

The purpose of this book is to facilitate travel, one purpose of which is to try exciting new things. Shopping-mall food is the reverse of a new thing. It's a sure thing and, food-wise, usually a sure-to-be mediocre thing. However, certain ancillary considerations—among them comfort, convenience, and economy—make the contemporary American shopping malls one of the most expedient institutions to lately appear on the travel horizon.

Malls are everywhere. They started in the suburbs, but every city worth its weight in quiche has now built a new mall or converted old structures for the purpose. Newer malls in several much visited U.S. cities are conveniently close to major attractions. Herald Center in New York is a block from the Empire State Building and Madison Square Garden. The Gallery is minutes away from Philadelphia's most prominent historic sights. Copley Place in Boston, Watertower Place in Chicago, and Embarcadero Center in San Francisco are all located near the heart of town.

Malls have much to offer the harried traveler. The comfort-controlled indoor climate is, as necessity dictates, warmer, cooler, and drier than external conditions. Admission is free, and malls are equipped with benches and washrooms that are usually quite clean and comfortable. Malls always have shops where travelers can obtain essential items—clothes, toiletries, and souvenirs.

Malls are also good places to grab a meal. Most contemporary malls have a multitude of diverse concessions surrounding a central seating area. For the traveler, this arrangement has several distinct advantages.

You can get virtually *any kind of food you want* at a mall. Every food area has a burger stand, a Chinese stand, tacos, pizza, pasta, a bakery, a deli, and even a health-food place with yogurt and salads. Some even serve alcohol. Grand Avenue Mall in Milwaukee, for example, serves beer, wine, and mixed drinks. In addition to voluptuous variety, the mall spares co-travelers the onerous task of reaching a consensus. Tom can devour a Philly cheese steak while Dick guzzles gazpacho and Harry nibbles a blondie.

Shopping-mall food clusters have no waitresses. No waitresses means even more than no tips. It means no innocent working stiff to deprive of a livelihood by commandeering a table. Like fast-food outlets anywhere, malls are great places to peruse maps or guidebooks or check out the local paper because, as long as you're quiet and look reasonably respectable, nobody kicks you out.

Travelers can, with ample justification, bemoan the replacement of neighborly shops and funky beaneries with shopping malls that look almost exactly the same anywhere you go. A rich part of the travel experience has been lost, never to be recaptured. But sometimes travelers need a respite from self-imposed demands to constantly experience, appreciate, and relate. And when they do, a familiar, impersonal, clean, antiseptic mall is usually near at hand.

OFF-PEAK BARGAINS

Like other travel-industry entities, restaurants charge less during slow times and more during busy periods.

Breakfast Specials

Breakfast specials are great bargains in many large cities. The New York breakfast is a legendary deal. Virtually every coffee shop, doughnut stand, and diner in Fund City (sic) offers breakfast specials for next to nothing. Specials consist of eggs, pancakes, toast, juice, and sometimes coffee offered in various permutations; costs range from $1.25 to $2. These deals are usually available in New York, Chicago, and a few other cities only until 10:30 or 11:00 A.M.

The Chinese Lunch

All Chinese restaurants serve lunch specials that usually include soup, an entrée with rice, tea, and a fortune cookie for from $3 to $5. Just make sure you order from the special lunch menu printed on a separate card or on the back of the regular menu. If you order from the regular menu, you may pay twice the price of the luncheon platter for an entree alone. Deals like this may be available in other types of Oriental restaurants and, indeed, in restaurants of any ilk, but you can bank on finding them in Chinese restaurants.

Dinner Time

It's hardly surprising that dinner is the most difficult meal to save money on. It's usually a restaurant's most profitable meal and its main reason for existing. A few restaurants offer discount prices on early dinners—either special menus or a percentage off regular prices. Since these deals tend to be temporary or promotional, the best way to find them is through ads in local papers and signs outside the businesses themselves.

Happy Hour

The most pleasant way to scrounge a cheap dinner is to participate in the great institution known as cocktail hour (a.k.a. happy hour, mood realignment period, and others). While most bars charge cut rates for drinks, the free hors d'oeuvres are the real enticement. Free eats that range from bowls of goldfish crackers to buffet tables groaning with hot chicken wings, tempura, and crudités can be yours for the price of a beer. As more states and communities pass legislation banning cheap or free drinks during happy hour, spreads are likely to become even more lavish.

Happy hours are widely advertised in local publications and on-premise signs. And while we normally shun the high prices and mediocre fare served by name-brand hotels, bigger hotels tend to have the most well-endowed happy hours. A drink in a top-flight hotel lounge may run upwards of $3, but that price may include unlimited passes at a sumptuous buffet table. Cocktail time is also a pleasant time to mingle with natives and fellow travelers. In fact, when it comes to drinks, food, and social opportunity, the ubiquitous happy hour is one of the happiest bargains around.

SEVEN

MONEY MATTERS

CHARGE CARDS

Yes, it is *possible* to travel without charge cards these days, but it sure isn't easy. Charge cards equal instant identity and instant credit. Without them, nobody knows who you are and you have to carry copious amounts of currency or traveler's checks to settle the tab.

Within the United States or abroad it's difficult to rent a car, cash a check, or check into a hotel without a charge card. You can use charge cards to access cash on the road. And they provide a record, offer some sort of recourse in the event of a dispute, and, overseas, usually fetch a more favorable exchange rate than cash or traveler's checks.

Plastic Money

There are two breeds of plastic money: travel and entertainment (T&E) cards—essentially American Express and Diners Club; and bankcards—Visa and MasterCard.

T&E cards memberships cost from $45 to $55 a year and have no spending limits, but you must settle the entire bill within thirty days (although both American Express and Diners Club have optional credit plans available).

Bankcards are issued by individual banks and savings-and-loan institutions. The issuing financial institution determines how much the cards cost (from nothing to $35 a year), the customer's credit limit, and which of a host of free or extra-charge "enhancements" are included with the card. Credit terms are dictated by the state in which the issuing bank—not the card holder—is located.

In early 1986, the Sears Financial Network introduced the Discover Card as a major contender to the credit-card scene. Like Visa and MasterCard, it is a credit card that charges interest (19.8 percent annually) on the unpaid balance. Unlike most bankcards, however, there is at present *no annual fee* for obtaining the card.

Although the Discover Card lacks the deep penetration of the established cards, it is accepted by many major airlines, car-rental firms, hotel chains, and restaurants. It can be used to access cash at 5,000 automatic-teller machines and to cash checks of up to $250 at Sears stores. Discover also pays dividends of up to 1 percent of total annual purchases; this dividend can be used to settle current balances, buy Sears gift certificates, or for deposits in a Discover

Savers' money-market account. To apply for a Discover Card, call 800-858-5588.

Charge-Card Acceptance

As long as airlines, hotels, restaurants, car renters, and other businesses accept it, the difference between cards is strictly between the card holder and card issuer. But card-issuer economics do influence how widely cards are accepted. *An increasing number of establishments will accept only bankcards*, and it's easy to understand why. Since card holders pay no interest, T&E cards make most of their profit on the percentage of sales they retain from the merchant. Consequently, T&E cards retain a much higher percentage of the bill than do bankcards.

The optimum situation is to carry one T&E card (for unlimited credit) and one bankcard (for universal acceptance). Within these categories, I recommend American Express for its array of collateral financial services and Visa for its wide acceptance, particularly in Europe.

Obtaining Charge Cards

To obtain a T&E card, you must apply to the company itself: for American Express, call 800-THE CARD; Diners Club, 800-CLUB INFO (yes, there *is* one digit too many but the final "O" doesn't count).

Bankcards can be obtained from a local bank or savings and loan or from one of the big national banks—Citibank, First National of Chicago, Bank of America. Some airlines (Alaska Air, American, Continental, Eastern, Piedmont, United) have forged alliances with card-issuing banks. Whenever customers charge any purchase to such cards, they receive mile-per-dollar-spent credit on the airline's frequent-flyer program. Holiday and Sheraton also issue bankcards; TWA and Northwest have similar arrangements with Diners Club.

Several non-profit organizations issue bankcards that forward a percentage of charges or flat per-purchase fees to the organization. Such cards include the Nuclear Free America's Working Assets Visa Card (325 E. 25th St., Baltimore, MD 21218; 301-235-3575); the Sierra Club Visa Card (730 Polk St., San Francisco, CA 94109; 415-776-2211); Cystic Fibrosis Visa Card (800-445-1336); Vietnam Veterans of America Visa Card (800-338-VETS, ext. 101).

Since there is no particular advantage to having a card issued by a local bank, it makes sense to shop for your card in the national marketplace. Compare yearly costs, interest rates, minimum payments and such enhancements as card registrations, insurance, luggage and key registration, message service, and hotel and car-rental discounts.

Some banks charge *no annual fee*, hoping to make it up on the interest payments imposed on the unpaid balance. If you are the type of customer who pays the entire bill each month, this is the deal for you. To obtain a complete list of banks that offer no-fee charge cards, send $1.95 to Bankcard Holders of America, 333 Pennsylvania Avenue S.E., Washington D.C. 20003.

PLASTIC SURGERY:
CHARGE-CARD REFERRAL AGENTS

Not everyone receives a wholehearted welcome to the international plastic market. Those who have lousy credit or no credit, are recently out of school, or new on a job may be rejected for the T&E cards and bankcards. For the time being, these unfortunates might as well forget about T&E cards. However, if you are among the rejected, you do have a good, albeit unconventional shot at obtaining a bankcard.

There is a new mini-industry of firms that match not-so-hot credit risks with banks and savings-and-loan institutions in search of more business. These outfits refer to themselves as bankcard service centers or referral agents, and they are easy to find. Their classified ads run daily in the Commercial Notices section of major newspapers under such exclamatory headings as "Credit!" "Get Visa or MasterCard!" or "Credit Cards Now Available!" The rest of the ad offers previous rejects an astounding rate of acceptance, usually 98 percent, by applying with them.

What these outfits do is solicit and screen applicants on behalf of banks and savings-and-loan institutions. A Chatsworth, California, company called Service One Corporation, for example, represents Home Trust Savings of Vermillion, South Dakota; People's Credit of New York represents Key Savings & Loan, no location given. And while these firms usually deliver what they advertise, their business methods seem evasive and the card you get is less than it appears to be.

Collateral Savings Accounts

To apply for a card, you must first pay the agent a fee, usually $25 to $50, which may or may not be refundable if your application is refused. If your application is approved, you must then open a *collateral savings account* at the card-issuing financial institution. Each deal requires a minimum deposit ranging from $250 to $500 per card and all of them stipulate a maximum deposit of $2,500.

The big chill arrives when you realize that *the amount in your savings account represents your total credit limit.* If you have $300 in your account, you can charge no more than $300 worth of travel—hardly enough to wander very far from home. The issuing institution can afford to grant cards to credit risks because it already has their payments on deposit. If you need to close your savings account, you can do so only after you have paid off the balance on the charge card and have returned the card to the issuing institution.

Collateral savings accounts pay *minimal interest*, about 5¼ percent. Also, the banks issuing these cards are usually located in states like South Dakota, which allow card issuers to charge the *highest interest on the unpaid balance.*

At the end of the year the financial institution usually reviews the card holder's credit record and decides whether the collateral savings account must be maintained and if the credit limit may be increased.

Other Fees and Costs

Along with the amount of compulsory deposit, other qualifications vary. People's Credit of New York requires applicants to have a minimal annual income of $9,600, no current credit problems, and no rectified credit problems or bankruptcies during the previous four years. J&B Financing Service of Southfield, Michigan, requires a $10,000 income and "good credit during the last 12 months." A New York City agent refuses only recent bankrupts and those who have already accrued substantial debts to Visa or MasterCard.

Another aspect to compare in choosing a bankcard is the *agency fee.* People's Credit wants a $25 nonrefundable fee to receive an application and another $25 nonrefundable fee when you apply. Service One wants a onetime $40 "processing fee," which it will return if your application is refused. The individual bank determines the annual fee for its cards (usually $25 to $35), and its state of residence sets interest rates for unpaid balances (18 to 22 percent).

The Plastic Imperative

Using bankcard agents or referral services costs more than going directly through a bank or savings-and-loan institution. But they can help otherwise un-card-worthy individuals obtain a semblance of a bankcard which, travel-wise, is a monumental improvement over having none at all. Even if you never use the card for major travel expenses—and with a $250 to $300 limit how major can they be?—a charge card is valuable.

Use the card to *cash checks* or for *identification* when paying by check, to *rent cars* (even if you ultimately pay by check or cash), *guarantee hotel reservations, check into hotels, access spot cash, or obtain assistance for other emergencies.

Use the card to charge an *unlimited amount of minor expenditures*. Since merchants usually don't call the card company for authorization on purchases of less than $50, small purchases don't count against your credit limit.

Obtaining a card issued by the Boondocks National Bank also helps you to *establish a credit history*, which is necessary if you are to qualify for a standard—no collateral savings account–bankcard or T&E card.

The disadvantages are the fees and the collateral account. If you already have a couple of thousands sitting in a low-interest savings account, it's no great hardship to maintain a similar account in South Kishnev. Just remember that if you have to close the account for any reason, they perform a plastic-ectomy.

The main point is that *not* having a charge card is the travel equivalent of spitting in the wind. If a referral agent/collateral savings account is your only route to a Visa or MasterCard, make the call, pay the fee, put up the collateral—then take the plastic and run.

━━━━━━━━━━━━ ◈ TRAVELER'S ALERT ◈ ━━━━━━━━━━━━

Charge-card referral agents usually deliver what they promise, but their professional practices seldom inspire a high degree of confidence. Most of their advertising lists only long-distance phone numbers, no addresses. These numbers usually turn out to be answering services; ask to speak to a company official and they will either admit they are services or say that the credit representative just stepped out of the office. And although the material you receive seldom lists phone numbers and addresses, a post-office box or private mail-receiving service is usually indicated.

Regarding these plastic-for-everybody offers, a Subject Report prepared by the Better Business Bureau of Metropolitan New York warns that "consumers should be wary of companies whose claims are 'too good to be true' . . . Not only were such claims false, but in some cases exorbitant fees were being charged for credit information generally available to the public at little or no charge. In several cases the U.S. Postal Service stepped in and put a stop to such practices." Consider yourself forewarned.

PAYING THE BILL

While finding off-price travel deals is most of the battle, the way you pay determines the full final cost. There are four principal ways of settling travel expenses—cash, traveler's checks, charge cards, and personal checks—each with its attendant pecuniary and psychic fees.

"Use charge cards whenever possible while traveling abroad: Charges are normally converted at an exchange rate more favorable than you could get for traveler's checks or cash."

Charge Cards

My personal rule of thumb for settling travel expenses is to *use charge cards whenever possible*. There's no really good reason not to. If you use a travel and entertainment card or pay your bankcard bill at the end of the month, charges cost no more than cash. But in several significant respects, charging may save you both money and aggravation.

● *You don't pay right away.* It may be a month or more before you see a bill, during which time your money—assuming you already have it—is earning interest in a savings or checking account. If you don't have it, you at least have some time to get it.

● *Overseas, paying with a charge card is cheaper than paying cash because card companies get better exchange rates than individuals.* Individuals convert cash or traveler's checks at the retail exchange rate. When bills are charged in a foreign currency, the charge-card company converts it at the more favorable wholesale exchange rate.

Even though American Express and Diners Club tack on a 1 percent surcharge and bankcards add markups of various amounts, the marked-up exchange rate is still better than what you would have received by exchanging cash or traveler's checks. This may not hold true if the value of the dollar decreases between the day of purchase and the day the company processes the bill. On the other hand, you reap windfall savings if the dollar rises during the lag time.

Other Plastic Virtues

● Charge cards decrease both the inconvenience and possible risks involved in carrying cash, buying traveler's checks, or, when traveling abroad, exchanging currency.

● Charge cards provide records and verification for purposes of tax deduction or reimbursement.

● When you buy air, rail, or bus tickets, all charge-card companies provide free accident insurance in varying amounts to cover you while you are in transit.

● Use of charge cards provides a certain amount of recourse in the event of a dispute. If you have a complaint against an airline, hotel, or travel agent, you can present your case to the charge-card company for adjudication prior to paying the bill.

Traveler's Checks

One major advantage of traveler's checks is that they can be replaced quickly when lost or stolen. Another is that because they are easier for banks to process, traveler's checks frequently fetch a better foreign-exchange rate than cash.

Among the disadvantages is the fact that despite what Karl Malden or any other hired spokesperson tells you, *traveler's checks are not the same as cash*. To my knowledge, no restaurant or shop has ever refused to accept cash; no merchant requires customers to show identification before paying cash; no proprietor looks at you as if you've asked permission to rifle the cash register if you spend cash. But they—ever more frequently—do all of these things if you try to use traveler's checks.

Traveler's checks usually cost 1 percent of the amount purchased, although some banks offer them free to account holders. (Diners Club card holders qualify for no-fee Citicorp traveler's checks.) The fee is low because traveler's checks issuers profit on the "float"—the interest your money earns them between the time you buy the check and the time you cash it.

You can also buy traveler's checks in foreign currencies before you leave the country from dealers such as Deak Perera. But doing so doesn't really expedite the cashing process and only gambles that the value of the dollar will fall before you use the checks.

Cash

The big advantage of cash is universal no-questions-asked acceptance. The big drawback is universal danger of loss or theft. Minimize the risk of carrying cash with a few tried-and-true crime-stopper tricks:

● Don't keep all your cash in one place; distribute it among different pockets of your clothes.
● Don't put cash into a checked suitcase.
● Don't leave cash in a hotel room—use the hotel safe.
● Beware of crowds.

Many ingenious products have been devised for inconspicuously carrying cash and other low-bulk valuables: money belts, money holsters, money socks, for example. To receive a catalog showing the latest fashions in cashware and other hard-to-find travel gadgets, send $.50 to: Travelers Checklist, Cornwall Bridge Road, Sharon, CT 06069; 203-364-0144.

Personal Checks

The last and least advisable way to pay is by writing a personal check, which, even when accepted, must usually be accompanied by a charge card, passport, or other airtight ID. You're most likely to use them at certain hotels, particularly down-scale properties and small bed & breakfast operations that do not accept charge cards but will take suitably verified personal checks.

Even if you don't plan to pay for anything by check, bring a few checks on any trip in case of the unexpected. Checks are especially handy if you run out of cash. American Express offices cash checks, and many hotels and rent-a-car desks will cash customers' personal checks when accompanied by a charge card.

FOREIGN EXCHANGE

Where you exchange currency can make a big difference in what you get for it. Like every other element of the travel industry, the foreign-exchange industry exploits travelers who don't plan and won't shop. Here are some guidelines for finding favorable exchange rates.

● *Exchange currency after you enter the country rather than before you arrive.* Exchanging abroad eliminates the extra costs for shipping, handling, and overhead that accrue to any imported commodity—even cold, hard cash. However, try to have a nominal amount of foreign currency on hand—$25 to $50—when you enter a new country, at least enough to allow you to bypass the long lines and unfavorable rates at airport-exchange offices and get into the city.

● *The best exchange rates are usually available at large commercial banks; the worst rates at airports.* While many hotels exchange money as a convenience to guests, they discourage the practice by offering unfavorable rates. The rates offered by independent exchange dealers, such as those located throughout the tourist areas of London, generally fall somewhere between those offered by the big banks and the hotels.

● *Beware of firms with large "spreads" between the price for buying and selling a particular currency.* If the posted rates between the "buy" price and the "sell" price are more than about 5 percent, they are offering a bad buying rate, a bad selling rate, or bad rates for both.

● *The worst way to exchange money is to use foreign currency to pay for a restaurant check, hotel bill, or retail purchase.* These establishments willingly accept U.S. currency at 10 to 15 percent below regular exchange rates, and they return your change at the same low rate.

● *Keep in mind that the foreign-exchange rate listed in newspapers is not the rate consumers get.* The newspaper rate represents the wholesale rate applicable to large amounts of funds transferred by banks and other financial institutions. This rate varies by several percentage points and is never in your favor.

CASH ACCESS

It costs money to get money while you travel. But play your cards right—travel and entertainment cards, bankcards, and automatic teller-machine (ATM) cash cards—it won't cost that much.

American Express Options

American Express offers its card holders the most extensive range of cash access options available. Card holders can cash personal checks at any of nearly 1,200 American Express Travel Service offices in 480 U.S. cities and 130 countries. Green-card holders can receive up to $1,000 ($200 in local currency and $800 in traveler's checks, with 1 percent commission); gold-card holders can access up to $5,000 ($500/$4,500). Card holders can cash one check a week within the United States and one every twenty-one days overseas. Gold-card holders can also cash checks for up to $1,000 a week at any of the 2,000 U.S. banks that issue the gold card.

Outside of the travel offices, American Express card holders can cash checks for up to $250 per stay at hotels that accept American Express in the United States and Canada; and up to $100 at hotels outside North America. Certain airline ticket counters (American, Eastern, PSA, United) will cash personal checks of up to $50 for card holders holding tickets valid within forty-eight hours of the time the check is presented. Budget, American-International, Alamo, and Dollar car-rental desks will cash $50 checks for card holders with car-rental agreements valid within forty-eight hours.

An even easier way to get cash with an American Express card is by using one of the 11,000 Express Cash ATMs located in airports, hotels, shopping centers, American Express travel offices, or piggyback on cash machines operated by local banks. Card holders can access up to $500 in cash (for a $1.50 per transaction fee) and $500 in traveler's checks (with a 1 percent commission) every seven days. (There is an additional 1 percent fee for international cash transactions.)

To enroll in the program, card holders must choose a Personal Identification Number (PIN) and designate a checking account from which cash access and purchases by traveler's check are directly debited. To locate cash machines, participants can consult a directory of machine locations or call a twenty-four-hour, seven-day a week toll-free hotline: 800-227-4669 (800-CASH-NOW).

Members of the Diners Club "Club Cash" program can obtain funds at 16,000 Plus System, Instant Cash, Metroteller, Minibank, $AM, MPACT, and Presto! ATMs. Diners Club card holders can also cash checks of up to $250 per stay at properties in fifty hotel chains and up to $1,000 at 1,700 branches of Citibank in more than seventy countries ($50 per check minimum within the United States; $250 minimum overseas; 1 percent service charge with a $5 per check minimum).

The Discover Card can access up to $500 at 17,000 nationwide ATMs and Sears stores.

Automatic Teller-Machine Networks

Within the United States and Canada, the most convenient and cheapest way to access cash is to use an automatic teller machine operated by the bankcards, Discover, and either of two nationwide bank networks, CIRRUS or Plus System. If your bankcard offers this enhancement, or you have a cash card issued by an ATM-system member bank, you can access cash at any of the thousands of facilities operated nationwide. Individual banks set cash limits and impose per-transaction fees ranging from zero to $1. Some bankcards charge instant interest on both cash advances and all other purchases made in the following billing period.

Of the two nationwide bank networks, CIRRUS is the larger—with 4,100 member financial institutions, 24,000 ATMs, and an estimated 97,000,000 card holders. To find out which banks in your area issue CIRRUS cards or, if you already have a card, request a directory or locate the nearest CIRRUS outlet, call the twenty-four–hour toll-free hotline: 800-4-CIRRUS (800-424-7787).

The Plus System has 2,000 member financial institutions and more than 16,700 machines in forty-eight states, Canada, Puerto Rico, the United Kingdom, and Japan. To locate the nearest Plus System bank or ATM, call 800-THE-PLUS (800-843-7587).

Both networks have forged alliances with the major bankcards:

Cirrus + MasterCard
Plus System + Visa

If your bankcard has issued you a PIN, you may be able to use your MasterCard or Visa to access cash at a Cirrus or Plus System ATM.

However, before these great alliances came to pass, individual card-issuing banks had already established arrangements with Cirrus or Plus System. Consequently, some Visa cards access Cirrus ATMs and some MasterCards access Plus System equipment. What's a cardholder to do? Look at the back of your bankcard: The symbol you see is the ATM network you get.

Bankcard Cash Advances

The worst and most expensive way to access spot cash is to get a cash advance on a Visa or MasterCard. First, it is inconvenient. You must perform this transaction at a bank during elusive "normal banking hours" and wait while the bank that issued your card authorizes the advance.

Second, it is expensive. The cash advance is considered a loan, and you are charged the normal interest rate on unpaid balances —between 18 and 22 percent annually—from the moment you receive the funds. There is no thirty-day grace period on repaying a cash advance; the next bankcard bill you receive will include interest for it.

Getting cash on the road can be easy and cheap—if you carry the right cards and bring along some blank checks. Running short of cash without them can quickly escalate into emergency scenarios involving Western Union money orders, international bank transfers, American consulates, and other extreme measures too horrible and, for the most part, unnecessary to contemplate.

DIALING FOR FEWER DOLLARS
Hotels

Lesson number one for cutting costs on phone calls made on the road: *Don't charge long-distance calls to your hotel bill.*

A lesser-known species of deregulation with no felicitous results for travelers involves hotel surcharges for interstate long-distance calls. Previously, hotels could only pass along Bell System rates. But as of June 1981, the Federal Communications Commission permits hotels to resell interstate long-distance service they receive from Bell or one of its competitors at any price they choose. Suddenly the bedside telephone has become yet another hotel profit center.

"Be aware that the hefty surcharge many hotels levy on long-distance telephone calls often applies to credit-card and toll-free calls."

Hotel long-distance surcharges assume various disguises. Some hotels impose flat charges ranging from $.50 to $1.25 per direct-dialed call regardless of the cost of the call. Others charge higher rates for the call itself, often imposing the operator-assisted daytime rate on direct-dialed calls placed at any hour. Some hotels levy an incremental surcharge of 10 to 30 percent above the operator-assisted direct-dial rate. If you actually do use the assistance of an operator, you pay even more.

Hotel chains usually leave surcharge policies to the discretion of local management. You cannot assume that the surcharge will be the same in every Marriott, Holiday Inn, or Red Roof Inn. The only way to find out is to ask the hotel itself; the toll-free reservation number probably won't be up on this.

Avoid the hotel surcharge completely by charging calls—to a Bell system calling card or home phone, or by calling collect. You'll pay operator-assisted rates but get off-hour discount rates and beat the hotel surcharge. If you place the call from your room, the hotel may still impose a hefty service charge. To avoid even this expense, make the call from a pay phone in the lobby.

Alternative Long-Distance Services

Several of the alternative long-distance phone systems—GTE Sprint, I.T.T., Skyline, MetroFone—offer major savings on calls made away from home. By using local access numbers in most large cities or national toll-free numbers, subscribers pay a surcharge, but get the same rates for calls made from the road as they would for calls made at home. This compares very favorably with Bell calling-card rates, for which you pay operator-assisted rates even if you self-dial. Phones with direct access to several of the major long-distance services are located in many airports.

If you place an alternative-system call from a hotel room, you will have to pay for the local call to the access number. Calling the access number from suburban or outlying locations can run up considerable charges from a hotel phone. You may still benefit by placing alternative-service calls from a hotel lobby.

─────────◇ TRAVELER'S ALERT ◇─────────

Use hotel-room telephones as seldom as possible. Local calls can be expensive—up to $1 in some hotels. And many hotels impose service charges of up to $1 on 800-number calls that would be free if made from pay phones in the hotel lobby.

Timing Is Money

"To place phone calls to Europe, call before 7 A.M., normal business hours there, and the lowest rate period here."

When calling long distance away from home or planning a trip, proper timing means substantial savings. The Bell System and most of its competitors have a three-tier pricing system on long-distance calls. The full rate is charged for calls placed between 8:00 A.M. and 5:00 P.M. on weekdays; a 35 percent off evening rate is in effect between 5:00 P.M. and 11:00 P.M. Sunday through Friday; and the 60 percent off night rate is charged between 11:00 P.M. and 8:00 A.M. every day, all day Saturday, and on Sunday until 5:00 P.M.

During normal 9:00 to 5:00 business hours, the rate system offers a few breaks for calls across time zones. Travelers in the Eastern time zone get one hour of business-day calls at evening rates to the Central time zone, two hours to the Mountain time zone, and three to the Pacific time zone. Pacific time zone callers get an even better deal calling east in the morning. They can make business-day calls to the Eastern time zone between 6:00 A.M. and 8:00 A.M. at the lowest night rates. Ma Bell even facilitates these savings schemes by including area code and time-zone maps in its directories.

For calls to Europe, full rates are charged only between 7:00 A.M. and 1:00 P.M. There is a 25 to 30 percent discount between 1:00 P.M. and 6:00 P.M.; and a 40 to 45 percent discount between 6:00 P.M. and 7:00 A.M. The same rates apply every day of the week.

Since Europe is between five (United Kingdom, Ireland) and seven (Greece, Finland, Israel) hours ahead of the Eastern time zone, you can reach Europe during their business day at our cheapest rates by making early-morning calls from anywhere in the United States. And European early mornings correspond to the wee hours in the Far West. To receive "AT&T International Dialing," a free brochure containing complete information on foreign rates, time zone, and dialing codes, call the AT&T International Information Service: 800-874-4000.

Other Dial-for-Fewer-Dollars Stratagems

• Since most airlines and hotels are always open, call them at the cheapest possible times.

• Save pay-phone charges on local calls by using 800 numbers whenever possible. For example, airlines with local service often also have toll-free numbers you can call. (Both numbers access the same reservations office.) Call toll-free information (for free) at 800-555-1212 to check it out.

● Many people are not aware that the higher evening rate—not the low night rate—applies to calls made after 5:00 P.M. on Sunday.

● Similarly, daytime calls on five legal holidays—Christmas, New Year's, Independence Day, Labor Day, and Thanksgiving—are charged evening rates not, as many people mistakenly believe, night rates. Daytime calls placed on other weekday holidays are not subject to discount.

● If the rate period changes during a call, you are charged a dual rate. Only the first minute of a call placed at 7:59 A.M. on Tuesday morning, for example, qualifies for the cheap night rate.

APPENDIX

TOLL-FREE NUMBERS

These are the most widely applicable toll-free numbers operated by each travel company. If any of these numbers fail to work from your calling area, call toll-free information at 800-555-1212.

1. AIRLINES

Aer Lingus	800-223-6537
Aeromexico	800-AEROMEX
Air Canada	800-4-CANADA
Air France	800-237-2747
Air Jamaica	800-523-5585
Air Virginia	800-446-7834
Air Wisconsin	800-247-9472
Alitalia	800-223-5730
Allegheny Commuter	800-428-4253
Alaska Airlines	800-426-0333
ALM Antillean	800-327-7230
America West Airlines	800-247-5692
American Airlines	800-433-7300
Braniff	800-BRANIFF
British Airways	800-247-9297
British Caledonian	800-231-0270
Britt Airways	800-652-7488
Business Express	800-345-3400
BWIA International	800-432-5621
Canadian Airlines International (CP Air)	800-426-7000
Challenge Air	800-343-1222
City Express	800-387-3060
ComAir	800-354-9822
Continental Airlines	800-525-0280
Delta Air Lines	800-221-1212
Eastern Airlines	800-EASTERN
Empire Airlines	800-448-4104
Finnair	800-223-5700
Iberia	800-221-9741
Icelandair	800-223-5500
Japan Air Lines	800-525-3663
KLM	800-556-7777
Korean Air	800-421-8200
Lufthansa	800-645-3880
Mexicana	800-531-7921

Midway Airlines	800-621-5700
Midwest Express	800-452-2022
Northwest Orient (domestic)	800-225-2525
(international)	800-447-4747
Pan Am	800-442-5896
Piedmont Airlines	800-251-5720
Precision Airlines	800-451-4221
Qantas	800-227-4500
Quebecair	800-361-4940
Scandinavian Air Systems	800-221-2350
Swissair	800-221-4750
TWA (domestic)	800-221-2000
(international)	800-892-4141
United Airlines	800-241-6522
USAir	800-428-4322
Varig	800-468-2744
Virgin Atlantic	800-862-8621

2. RENT-A-CARS

Agency	800-221-8666
Ajax	800-352-2529
Alamo	800-327-9633
American International	800-527-0202
Avis	800-331-1212
Budget	800-527-0700
Dollar	800-421-6878
Enterprise	800-325-8007
General	800-327-7607
Hertz	800-654-3131
National	800-328-4567
Payless (formerly Holiday-Payless)	800-237-2804
Rent-A-Dent	800-426-5243
Rent-A-Wreck	800-421-7253
Rent Rite	800-243-7483
Snappy	800-321-7159
Thrifty	800-367-2277
Tropical	800-367-5140
Ugly Duckling	800-528-1584
United States Associated	800-323-3024
USA Car Rental	800-USA-CARS
Value	800-327-2501

3. TOURISM BUREAUS

Alabama	800-252-2262
Amarillo (TX)	800-692-1338
Arkansas	800-643-8383

Asheville (NC)	800-257-1300
Barbados	800-221-9831
Berkshire (MA) Visitors' Bureau	800-BERKSHR
Bermuda	800-BERMUDA
British Virgin Islands	800-835-8530
Buffalo	800-235-6979
California	800-TO-CALIF
Charleston, SC	800-545-7108
Colonial Williamsburg (VA)	800-HISTORY
Colorado	800-433-2656
Connecticut	800-243-1685
Costa Rica	800-762-5909
Daytona Beach	800-535-2828
Delaware	800-441-8846
El Paso (TX)	800-351-6024
Estes Park	800-621-5888
Fiji	800-621-9604
Fort Worth (TX)	800-433-5747
Hot Springs (AK)	800-643-1570
Houston	800-231-7799
Idaho	800-635-7820
Illinois	800-232-0121
Indiana	800-858-8073
Ireland	800-223-6470
Kentucky	800-225-8747
Kissimmee-St. Cloud (FL)	800-327-9159
Lake Tahoe	800-822-5922
Louisiana	800-334-8626
Louisville	800-626-5646
Massachusetts	800-248-5700
Michigan	800-543-2937
Minnesota	800-328-1461
Mississippi	800-647-2290
Mobile (AL)	800-662-1984
Montana	800-548-3390
Myrtle Beach (SC)	800-722-3224
Nebraska	800-228-4307
New Mexico	800-545-2040
New York State	800-CALL-NYS
Newfoundland & Labrador	800-563-6353
North Carolina	800-VISIT-NC
NC High Country Host	800-438-7500
North Dakota	800-437-2077
Northern Kentucky	800-354-9718
Nova Scotia	800-341-6096
Ohio	800-BUCKEYE

Oklahoma	800-CALL-OKL
Ontario	800-268-3735
Oregon	800-547-7842
Palm Beach County (FL)	800-952-0600
Pensacola (FL)	800-874-1234
Philadelphia	800-225-5745
Pigeon Forge (TN)	800-251-9100
Pocono Mountains (PA)	800-POCONOS
Rhode Island	800-556-2484
San Antonio (TX)	800-531-5700
Santa Fe (NM)	800-528-5369
Saskatchewan	800-667-7191
Shreveport-Bossier (LA)	800-551-8682
South Dakota	800-843-1930
Southern New England (CT, RI, MA)	800-242-1520
Southwest Idaho	800-635-5240
Thousand Islands (NY)	800-847-5263
Valley Forge Country (PA)	800-441-3549
Vermont	800-331-1750
Virginia	800-VISIT VA
Virginia Beach (VA)	800-446-8038
Washington (state)	800-541-9274
West Virginia	800-624-9110
Wisconsin	800-ESCAPES
Wyoming	800-443-2784
Zambia	800-223-5316

4. OTHER TOLL-FREE NUMBERS

Access International (off-price dealer)	800-584-4881
Airhitch	800-372-1234
Amtrak	800-872-7245
American Express	800-843-2273
AT&T International Information Service	800-874-4000
Council Charter	800-223-7402
Diners Club	800-258-2466
Discover Card	800-858-5588
Hilton Head Island (SC) Central Reservation Center	800-845-7018
Key West (FL) Reservation Service	800-327-4831
Maharaja Travels (off-price dealer)	800-835-9684
Maryland Reservation Center	800-654-9303
Mc Son Travel (off-price dealer)	800-622-1421
McTravel (fee-based travel agent)	800-331-2941
Meegan Services (hotel reservations nationwide)	800-221-1235

New York area airport ground transportation information	800-247-7433
Orlando Central Reservations Center	800-322-2220
Washington (D.C.) Central Reservation Center	800-554-2220

BOOKSELLERS

Although vast amounts of money-saving travel information can be obtained for free (see Chapter One), some knowledge is well worth paying for. Guidebooks are particularly useful for unearthing good hotel values and off-the-beaten-path restaurants, deciphering the local transit system, and apprehending other cost-cutting "secrets" known only to locals and other savvy travelers.

The major national bookstore chains—B. Dalton, Waldenbooks, Barnes & Noble, Crown—contain an admirable selection of travel books. Here is a list of catalog-order firms and stores (many of which also accept mail and phone orders) that specialize in travel books, maps, and travel-related accessories:

Catalogs
(*Indicates store located at this address)

Banana Republic Travel
  Bookstore
Box 7737
San Francisco, CA 94120
800-772-9977

*Book Passage
51 Tamal Vista
Corte Madera, CA 94925
800-321-9785; 415-927-0960

Bradt Enterprises
95 Harvey St.
Cambridge, MA 02140
617-492-8776

De Lorme's Map Store
Box 298
Freeport, ME 04032
800-227-1656; in ME
  800-462-0029

*Forsyth Travel Library
Box 2975
9154 W. 57th St.
Shawnee Mission, KS 66201
800-367-7984; in KS,
  913-384-3440

*Phileas Fogg's Books &
  Maps for the Traveler
87 Stanford Shopping Center
Palo Alto, CA 94304
800-533-3644; 415-327-1754

Wayfarer Books
P.O. Box 1121
Davenport, IA 52805
319-355-3902

Stores
ARIZONA
Banana Republic Travel
  Bookstore
2582-101 E. Camelback Rd.
Phoenix, AZ 85016
602-955-9108

Places & People
2623 N. Campbell Ave.
Tucson, AZ 85719
602-577-9620

Wide World of Maps
2626 W. Indian School Rd.
Phoenix, AZ 85017
602-279-2323

Wide World of Maps
1526 N. Scottsdale Rd.
Tempe, AZ 85281
602-949-1012

Wide World of Maps
1440 S. Country Club Dr.
Mesa, AZ 85202
602-844-1134

CALIFORNIA (Northern)
Banana Republic Travel
  Bookstore
224 Grant Ave.
San Francisco, CA 94108
415-433-2022

Easy Going
Shattuck Commons
1400 Shattuck Ave.
Berkeley, CA 94709
415-843-3533

Easy Going
1617 Locust
Walnut Creek, CA 94596
415-947-6660

European Book Store
925 Larkin St.
San Francisco, CA 94109
415-474-0626

Gourmet Guides
1767 Stockton St.
San Francisco, CA 94133
415-391-5903

The Map Center
2440 Bancroft Way
Berkeley, CA 94704
415-841-6277

Rand McNally Map Store
595 Market St.
San Francisco, CA 94105
415-777-3131

Sierra Club Book Store
730 Polk St.
San Francisco, CA 94109
415-923-5600

Sierra Club Book Store
6014 College Ave.
Oakland, CA 94618
415-658-7470

Sierra Club Book Store
Ocean Ave. & Dolores St.
Box 5667
Carmel, CA 93921
408-624-8032

Thomas Brothers Maps &
  Books
550 Jackson St.
San Francisco, CA 94133
415-981-7520

TravelMarket
Golden Gateway Commons
130 Pacific Avenue Mall
San Francisco, CA 94111
415-421-4080

The Travel Store
56½ N. Santa Cruz Ave.
Los Gatos, CA 95030
408-354-9909

CALIFORNIA (Southern)
Banana Republic Travel
  Bookstore
9669 Santa Monica Blvd.

Beverly Hills, CA 90210
213-858-7900

Banana Republic Travel
Bookstore
110 S. Hope Ave.
Santa Barbara, CA 93105
805-687-8988

Geographica Map & Travel
Book Store
4000 Riverside Dr.
Burbank, CA 91505
818-848-1414

John Cole's Book Shop
180 Prospect St.
La Jolla, CA 92037
619-454-4766

Map Centre Inc.
2611 University Ave.
San Diego, CA 92104
619-291-3830

Pacific Travellers Supply
529 State St.
Santa Barbara, CA 93101
805-963-4438

Plan-It Travel Store
777 S. Main St.
Orange, CA 92668
714-973-8979

Thomas Brothers Maps &
Books
603 W. 7th St.
Los Angeles, CA 90017
800-432-8430; 213-627-4018

Thomas Brothers Maps &
Books
17731 Cowan
Irvine, CA 92714
714-863-1984

Traveler's Depot
1539 Garnet Ave.
San Diego, CA 92109
619-483-1421

Le Travel Store
295 Horton Plaza
San Diego, CA 92101
800-854-6677; in CA,
619-544-0005

Travel Suppliers
727 N. Placentia Ave.
Fullerton, CA 92631
714-528-2502

COLORADO
Banana Republic Travel
Bookstore
1147 Pearl St.
Boulder, CO 80302
303-442-8250

Tattered Cover Book Store
2955 E. First Ave.
Denver, CO 80206
800-833-9327; in CO,
800-821-2896; 303-322-7727

CONNECTICUT
Banana Republic Travel
Bookstore
25 W. Farms Mall
Farmington, CT 06032
203-561-4360

DISTRICT OF COLUMBIA
Banana Republic Travel
Bookstore
3200 M Street NW
Washington, DC 20007
202-333-2584

The Map Store
1636 I Street NW
Washington, DC 20006
202-628-2608

Travel Merchandise Mart
1425 K Street NW
Washington, DC 20005
800-446-2424; in VA,
    800-572-1717; 202-371-6656

FLORIDA
Banana Republic Travel
    Bookstore
Town Center
Boca Raton, FL 33431
305-338-3490

The Map & Globe Store
1120 E. Colonial Dr.
Orlando, FL 32803
800-227-7538; 305-425-0185

The Map & Globe Store
2328 Apalachee Pkwy.
Tallahassee, FL 32301
904-656-7723

GEORGIA
Banana Republic Travel
    Bookstore
3393 Peachtree Road
Atlanta, GA 30326
404-231-4905

Latitudes
4400 Ashford Dunwoody
    Road
Atlanta, GA 30346
404-394-2772

Latitudes
3349 Peachtree Road NE
Atlanta, GA 30326
404-237-6144

ILLINOIS
Banana Republic Travel
    Bookstore
Woodfield Shopping Center
Schaumberg, IL 60173
312-519-1558

Rand McNally Map Store
23 E. Madison St.
Chicago, IL 60602
800-323-1887; 312-332-4627

Sandmeyer's Bookstore
714 S. Dearborn St.
Chicago, IL 60605
312-922-2104

The Savvy Traveler
50 E. Washington St.
Chicago, IL 60602
312-263-2100

IOWA
Travel Genie Map & Book
    Store
113 Colorado Ave.
Ames, IA 50010
515-292-1070

MARYLAND
Banana Republic Travel
    Bookstore
100 Main St.
Annapolis, MD 21401
301-268-0345

Passenger Stop
732 Dulaney Valley
Towson, MD 21204
301-821-5888

Travel Books Unlimited
4931 Cordell Ave.
Bethesda, MD 20814
301-951-8533

MASSACHUSETTS
Banana Republic Travel
    Bookstore
201 Newbury St.
Boston, MA 02116
617-267-3933

The Globe Corner Bookstore
1 School St.
Boston, MA 02108
800-358-6013; 617-523-6658

Harvard Square Map Store
40 Brattle St.
Cambridge, MA 02138
617-497-6277

MICHIGAN
Banana Republic Travel
   Bookstore
16822 Kercheval Ave.
Grosse Pointe, MI 48230
313-884-8304

The Map & Globe Store
1606 E. Michigan Ave.
Lansing, MI 48912
517-484-1978

MINNESOTA
Latitudes
3801 Grand Avenue S
Minneapolis, MN 55409
612-823-3742

The Map Store
348 N. Robert St.
St. Paul, MN 55101
612-227-1328

MISSOURI
Banana Republic Travel
   Bookstore
Union Station
St. Louis, MO 63101
314-621-6311

NEW JERSEY
Banana Republic Travel
   Bookstore
17 Palmer Square
Princeton, NJ 08542
609-921-8111

Geostat Map & Travel Center
910 N. Route 73
Marlton, NJ 08053
609-983-3600

Geostat Map & Travel Center
Routes 206 & 518
Skillman, NJ 08558
800-332-6277; in NJ,
   800-626-6277; 609-924-2121

NEW YORK
Banana Republic Travel
   Bookstore
205 Bleeker St.
New York, NY 10012
212-473-9570

Banana Republic Travel
   Bookstore
2376 Broadway
New York, NY 10024
212-874-3500

The British Travel Bookshop
   Ltd.
British Tourist Authority
40 W. 57th St.
New York, NY 10019
212-765-0898

The Complete Traveller
199 Madison Avenue
New York, NY 10016
212-685-9007

Hagstrom Map & Travel
   Center
57 W. 43rd St.
New York, NY 10036
212-398-1222

Rand McNally Map Store
150 E. 52nd St.
New York, NY 10022
212-758-7488

Traveller's Bookstore
22 W. 52nd St.
New York, NY 10019
212-664-0995

TraveLore Books
2 Elm St.
Huntington, NY 11743
516-673-6066

OREGON
Powell's Travel Store
701 SW 6th Ave.
Portland, OR 97204
503-223-7331

PENNSYLVANIA
Banana Republic Travel
    Bookstore
1716 Walnut St.
Philadelphia, PA 19124
215-725-2247

Banana Republic Travel
    Bookstore
51 St. Georges Road
Ardmore, PA 19903
215-642-3036

Geostat Map & Travel Center
125 S. 18th St.
Philadelphia, PA 19103
215-564-4700

Travel Bound Book Store
815 S. Aiken Ave.
Pittsburgh, PA 15232
412-681-4100

SOUTH CAROLINA
Michelin Guides & Maps
Bibendum Road at New Cut
    Road
Box 3305
Spartanburg, SC 29304
800-423-0485; 803-599-0850

TEXAS
Banana Republic Travel
    Bookstore
10000 Research Blvd.
Austin, TX 78758
512-346-0688

Banana Republic Travel
    Bookstore
Chelsea Market
4621 Montrose
Houston, TX 77006
713-526-7117

Home-Garden & Travel
    Bookstore
2476 Bolsover St.
Houston, TX 77005
713-527-0619

Home-Garden & Travel
    Bookstore
5868 Westheimer St.
Houston, TX 77057
713-789-2269

The Travel Collection
8235 Shoal Creek Blvd.
Austin, TX 78758
512-454-7151

VIRGINIA
The Book Gallery
1207 Emmet St.
Charlottesville, VA 22901
804-977-2892

The Book Gallery
1601 Willow Lawn Dr.
Richmond, VA 23230
804-673-9613

Travel Books
Route 9
Hillsboro, VA 22132
703-668-6101

Travel Merchandise Mart
2102 Crystal Plaza
Arlington, VA 22202
800-446-2424; in VA,
   800-572-1717; 703-685-1676

WASHINGTON
Banana Republic Travel
  Bookstore
508 Union St.
Seattle, WA 98101
206-622-2303

Metsker Maps of Seattle
702 First Ave.
Seattle, WA 98104
206-623-8747

Pioneer Maps
14125 N.E. 20th St.
Bellevue, WA 98007
206-746-3200

The Travel Accessories
  Market
1419 First Avenue
Seattle, WA 98101
206-447-9468

Wide World Books & Maps
401 N.E. 45th St.
Seattle, WA 98105
206-634-3453

ABOUT THE AUTHOR

Theodore Fischer was born in Chicago on the day after the Cubs' most recent World Series appearance. He attended high school in the Chicago area and received a degree in English Literature from the University of Michigan.

Fischer caught the travel bug when, as a Peace Corps volunteer stationed in Ghana, he rambled around West Africa as far as Timbuktu. Returning to Chicago Fischer subsisted on a flavorful stew of miscellaneous occupations—taxi driver, bartender, boutique owner, door-to-door pollster, election judge, substitute teacher—before joining the staff of *Playboy* magazine as an editorial researcher.

Since moving to New York in 1980, Fischer has been a full-time free-lance writer. He has written articles on business, sex, relationships, medicine, entertainment, and travel for magazines such as *Playboy, Family Circle, McCall's, TWA Ambassador, Frequent Flyer, Good Housekeeping, Mademoiselle, Newsweek International, Penthouse Forum, Diversion, Oui, Travel/Holiday,* and *Games*. He is the general editor of *The Holiday Guide* series.

Fischer has taught writing at Queens College and edited *Business Traveler's Report*, a monthly newsletter for cost-conscious business travelers. He also produced and hosted "Inside Travel," a free-wheeling weekly talk show—travel news, features, interviews, call-in—shown live on cable TV systems throughout Manhattan.

Fischer accumulated his *Cheap/Smart Travel* expertise by dint of the necessity to finance a compulsion for frequent New York getaways on a free-lance writer's insubstantial and uncertain earnings.

INDEX